MOTHER ANGELICA
ON GOD, HIS HOME, AND HIS ANGELS

Also by Mother Angelica:

Praying with Mother Angelica
Meditations on the Rosary, the Way of the
Cross, and Other Prayers

Mother Angelica on Christ and Our Lady

Mother Angelica on Suffering and Burnout

Mother Angelica's Quick Guide to the Sacraments

Mother Angelica's Answers, Not Promises

Mother Angelica on Prayer and Living for the Kingdom

MOTHER ANGELICA ON GOD, HIS HOME, AND HIS ANGELS

EWTN PUBLISHING, INC.
Irondale, Alabama

EWTN Publishing, Inc.
5817 Old Leeds Road, Irondale, AL 35210

Distributed by Sophia Institute Press, Box 5284, Manchester, NH 03108.

Library of Congress Cataloging-in-Publication Data

Names: M. Angelica (Mary Angelica), Mother, 1923-2016, author.
Title: Mother Angelica on God, his home, and his angels.
Description: Irondale, Alabama : EWTN Publishing, Inc., 2018.
Identifiers: LCCN 2017047945 | ISBN 9781682780480 (hardcover : alk. paper)
Subjects: LCSH: Catholic Church—Doctrines. | Theology, Doctrinal—Popular works.
Classification: LCC BX1754 .M13 2018 | DDC 230/.2—dc23 LC record available at https://lccn.loc.gov/2017047945

First printing

CONTENTS

EDITOR'S NOTE

This volume brings together for the first time *The Father's Splendor*, *Healing Your Faith vs. Faith Healing*, *Sons of Light*, *Before Time Began*, and *Inside the Kingdom*, five "mini-books" written by Mother Angelica and published by Our Lady of the Angels Monastery in the 1970s. Each section of this book corresponds to one of Mother's original mini-books. Taken together, they form a unique and beautiful work of spiritual wisdom and prayerful reverence.

Mother Angelica wrote these words on a pad of paper while in Adoration of the Blessed Sacrament in the chapel of her monastery in Irondale, Alabama. Her order, the Poor Clares of Perpetual Adoration, has been dedicated to the Blessed Sacrament since its founding, and so it is only fitting that Mother's written works were completed in His Presence.

By the mid-1970s, the Nuns of Our Lady of the Angels Monastery were printing as many as twenty-five thousand copies of these mini-books and others per day. This was truly a nascent mass-media operation, one that would lead to the creation of EWTN—the Eternal Word Television Network.

This book is a faithful representation of Mother Angelica's original work, with only the most basic corrections of printing errors, adjustments to formatting, and so on. You can be confident that you are reading an authentic presentation of the wisdom and spirituality of one of the most important figures in the history of Catholicism in America.

MOTHER ANGELICA
ON GOD, HIS
HOME, AND HIS
ANGELS

GOD THE FATHER

THE FATHER'S SPLENDOR

During His lifetime, Jesus gave me many examples of the Father's Attributes. He showed the Father's Mercy when He asked forgiveness for His enemies, the Father's Providence when He trusted Himself to the care of others, the Father's Love and Compassion when He healed the blind and lepers, and the Father's Power when He calmed the storm at sea.

By His life, death, and resurrection, He merited for me a participation in all of the Father's beautiful attributes. I have been called by the Father to be Holy, given the Way of Holiness by the Son, and given the Means to Holiness by the Spirit, that I may reflect every day in some way these Divine Attributes.

Jesus has told me to be perfect as my Heavenly Father is perfect, and that means I must share in a finite way in His perfections.

This is possible only because Jesus became Man and took within His Human Nature these attributes of the Father through the Power of the Holy Spirit. He promised me that I would do greater things than He did (John 14:12), because He would intercede with His Father on my behalf and send me His Spirit to teach me all things.

Jesus has asked me to be Merciful as my Father is Merciful, Compassionate as He is Compassionate, and to love my neighbor as much as the Father loves the Son: "I give you a new commandment — love one another just as I love you" (John 13:34). "As the Father has loved Me, so I have loved you" (John 15:9).

Through Jesus, and in Jesus, I have been called to be holy — with God's own Holiness. I must look at these marvelous Attributes and make them part of my daily life, as Jesus did, to glorify the Father and be transformed into another Christ on earth.

All during His life, Jesus was absorbed in His Father. He desired nothing but the Father's Will. He taught the Father's Love, and glorified the Father by all His works.

Jesus looked upon my misery and weakness and gave me His Holy Spirit to teach, direct, and fill me with Grace, Gifts, and a Divine Participation in His Nature, that I may share, in some way, in the very life of God.

St. Paul tells me in 2 Corinthians 3:18 that I must reflect Jesus like a mirror.

I am a mirror to my neighbor, and in that mirror he must see a reflection of Jesus. If that mirror is cloudy or distorted, Jesus' reflection will be so vague it will hardly be seen.

I must keep my mirror as clean and bright as possible so Jesus' Face will be clear and strong—so strong that the mirror disappears and everyone looking into it sees no one but Jesus.

I am called by the Father to reflect His Son, in whom the Holy Spirit manifested in a visible way the invisible attributes of God.

This seems to be an impossible dream except that Jesus Himself said, "I have given them the Glory You gave Me, that they may be one as we are one. With Me in them and You in Me, may they be so completely one that the world will realize that it was You who sent Me, and that I have loved them as much as You loved Me" (John 17:22-23).

The world will know that Jesus is truly God's Son by the reflection of His own attributes in my soul.

I must look and see what God is, and then keep the mirror of my soul clean and bright so what I see and contemplate may be reflected to my neighbor.

ON GOD, HIS HOME, AND HIS ANGELS

When my neighbor sees me being merciful when offended, compassionate with the faults of others, kind to everyone, calm in times of tension, loving when not loved in return, and full of joy — then he will know God lives — and Jesus is Lord of All.

I will ponder and see how the Attributes of God affect my life, and how I can have a share in their splendor.

The Divine Attributes seem to affect my life in different ways. Some fill me with such awe and wonder that my soul seems to rise above itself, above the petty mundane things in life that weigh it down.

The Father lets me share in other Attributes, such as Mercy, Compassion, Love, and Goodness, and these make me more like His Son.

In the Attributes I share, some seem to be just for me — Peace, Tranquility, Omnipresence; others affect my neighbor — Justice, Mercy, and Providence.

Some Attributes keep me aware of His Presence in His Creation: His Power in the wind, His Beauty in a sunrise, His Splendor manifested in the leaves blazing forth various colors in Fall, and His Changelessness in the mountains.

I am surrounded and permeated by His Essence, and held in creation by His Omnipotence.

My life is truly filled with God and I knew it not.

- His *Mercy* comforts me when I fall
- His *Providence* takes care when I worry
- His *Goodness* makes me good
- His *Power* upholds me
- His *Love* fills me
- His *Wisdom* is my guide
- His *Changelessness* gives me security
- His *Tranquility* makes me calm
- His *Majesty* fills me with awe
- His *Beauty* entrances me
- His *Joy* sustains me in sorrow
- His *Light* enlightens my path
- His *Omnipresence* surrounds me like a cloak
- His *Immanence* fills me through and through
- His *Transcendence* is above me like the warm sun
- His *Grandeur* thrills my soul
- His *Unity* brings all things together in Him

I lose myself like an atom in the universe, when I realize that this Great God loves me.

His *Power* pushes a tiny seed through the ground, His *Wisdom* designs its growth, His *Providence* nourishes it, His

Generosity makes it bear fruit, and His *Goodness* gives that fruit beauty, taste, and fragrance.

His *Goodness* gives a refreshing fragrance to a rose, an overwhelming beauty to a sunset, a pleasing harmony to music, various flavors to food, and a variety of textures to everything His *Power* has created.

When I sin, His *Justice* makes me fearful, His *Mercy* gives me hope, and His *Goodness* restores me to Grace.

His *Power* created me, His *Wisdom* knit me in my mother's womb; His *Providence* sustained me; His *Omnipotence* breathed a soul into my body; His *Goodness* brought me forth in a world of beauty and in a family filled with love.

His *Beauty* is manifest in flowers and field, His *Serenity* in the tranquility of the sea, His *Light* penetrates to the depths of my soul, and His *Changeless Love* enfolds me.

His *Omnipotence* is reflected in the vast size and distance of the sun, His *Changelessness* in its rays, and His *Intelligence* in the multitude of ways those rays work for my good.

His *Wisdom* sees every detail of my life; His *Providence* protects me; His *Mercy* forgives me; His *Goodness* brings good out of my mistakes; and His *Joy* fills my life with many oases to rest and take courage.

As I work and labor for my bread, His *Light* gives me ideas; His *Omnipotence* makes me creative; and His *Omnipresence* keeps me company in lonely hours.

His *Love* is always there when I feel unloving and unloved; His *Peace* is ever ready to fill my soul when I am disturbed; His *Justice* will take care of the persecutions I have suffered, and His *Compassion* assures me of His Love.

His *Wisdom* designed His creation; His *Power* brought it into being; His *Providence* disposes and orders all things in their proper place, and His *Goodness* gives it all to me.

PRAYER

O Lord and Father, Your Attributes make me humble and fill me with Joy. Let the contemplation of Your Splendor raise me above the things that weigh me down, make me realize the dignity You have given me and the heights to which you have called me. Let the reflection of Jesus in my soul touch my neighbor, that together we may give You Glory. Amen.

ON GOD, HIS HOME, AND HIS ANGELS

The Wisdom of God

God knows Himself and every created thing perfectly. Not a blade of grass or the tiniest insect escapes His eye. Wisdom is not a part of God as it is a part of me — it *is* God. Wisdom is the very Being of God.

No creature, not even the most exalted angel, can understand God or have perfect knowledge of Him. God alone knows Himself, and Wisdom reaches into the depths of God.

It follows that since God knows Himself perfectly and I exist only in Him, He also knows me perfectly.

He knows me so perfectly that it is impossible for Him to know me any better. All my actions, thoughts, and desires are before Him.

God does not know me *because* I exist — His constant thought of me *causes* me to exist.

God really knows me, and because He does, I am.

His Wisdom determines the path of thousands of known and unknown worlds in the universe. Each one races through space at fantastic speed, in the orbit marked out for it by God. Men and nations come and go but these giant masterpieces of His Wisdom go on with such precision that we can determine their speed to the second.

I think of all creation as a product of His Power, but it is also a manifestation of His Wisdom—from the tiniest weed to the most exotic flower in the wilds of an unexplored jungle—each is a perfect work of art, shouting aloud to my soul the Wisdom and Glory of the Lord.

My own soul is proof of His Infinite Wisdom, for He created it to His own image and likeness. What a marvel to behold! The most glorious sunset, the most ravishing landscape, and the beauty of the ocean, all fade into nothingness in comparison with the Wisdom of God as it manifested itself in the creation of my soul.

God's Wisdom and my wisdom are poles apart. For me, a thing must exist before I know it, but with God it is different—He must know it before it has existence.

God's Wisdom knew me long before I existed, and brought me into being, and sustains my every breath from moment to moment.

God, Who keeps everything in existence, knows every detail of His creation—knows it clearly without confusion or obscurity.

Not the smallest insect or molecule escapes His eye or His Providence.

He not only knows all my actions but my every desire and heartbeat. Nothing escapes Him, and nothing happens to me that He does not know, permit, or ordain.

My future lies before Him as clearly as the present moment. More than that, my whole life lay before Him clearly and distinctly before He created anything. From eternity He knew me and will continue to do so for all the millions and billions of ages to come.

The Wisdom of God is so great that He also knows exactly what I would think and do under every possible circumstance and situation, and He placed me in that state of life and situation best suited for my salvation.

This all-embracing knowledge extends to all possible creatures—all the creatures He could create but never will.

An All-Wise God loves me.

CONSIDERATION

I can draw great benefit for my soul when I think about His Wisdom. The contemplation of this Attribute fills my soul with awe, reverence, and a deep sense of His Grandeur. My God is no small God but a Great God indeed.

This Attribute produces within the depths of my soul a profound humility and a realization of my finiteness. All the wisdom and knowledge of all the Angels and men combined are as a grain of sand on the seashore compared to the knowledge and wisdom of my Father.

His Wisdom causes me an interior joy and peace when I begin to understand He is so wonderful. His perfect knowledge of me gives me comfort in times of sorrow, patience in times of pain, and security when I know I can address Him at any time, in any place, and speak to Him as a friend speaks to a friend.

When I feel sad at the thought of leaving the things of this world or losing them, I will look at these things in relation to God, and then I will realize their true value.

I have a tendency to judge everything in its relationship to me instead of the value it has in God's eyes. I cannot judge everything solely on its good or bad effect on me. I must go beyond appearances and seek the Wisdom of God through the eyes of Faith, and value everything as it is before God.

I will look at my neighbor and appreciate his value before God in whose image he was created, and not judge him by my feelings toward him.

ON GOD, HIS HOME, AND HIS ANGELS

PRAYER

O God, let the thought of Your Wisdom fill my soul with humble awe and an exalted joy at Your perfections.

SCRIPTURE

O Divine Wisdom, in You is the Spirit of Understanding: holy, one, manifold, subtle, eloquent, active, undefiled, sure, sweet, loving that which is good, quick, which nothing hindereth, beneficent, gentle, kind, steadfast, assured, secure, having all power, overseeing all things, and containing all spirits, intelligible, pure.

You are more active than all active things, and reach everywhere and penetrate everything by reason of Your Purity. You are the vapor of the Power of God, and a certain pure emanation of the Glory of Almighty God, and therefore no defiled thing comes to You.

You are the brightness of Eternal Light and the unspotted mirror of God's Majesty, and the image of His Goodness. And being but one, You can do all things; and remaining in Yourself the same, You renew all things, and through all nations You convey Yourself into holy souls and make friends of God and the prophets.

You are more beautiful than the sun, and above all the order of the stars; being compared with the light, You are found before it. For after this comes night, but You are never overcome by evil.

You reach, therefore, from end to end mightily, and order all things sweetly. (Wis. 7:22-30, Douay-Rheims)

The Providence of God

It is easy to identify the Wisdom of God with His wonderful Providence. God's Providence disposes and directs everything for His own Honor and Glory and the happiness and good of my soul.

All of His creation in some way contributes to my good. I look at the sun and find that it contributes to my well-being when it paints flowers various colors for my pleasure, hardens clay to make my dishes, and melts snow to swell the rivers, only to draw up the water by evaporation to fill clouds that rain upon the fields and prairies.

His Providence not only guides the pathway of galaxies—but determines the life and death process of bacteria in a drop of water.

ON GOD, HIS HOME, AND HIS ANGELS

He created everything and everyone for a reason—everything from an Angel to a dewdrop. All without exception He has foreseen and regulates to the smallest detail.

Every situation in my life, even the most painful, is ordered by His Providence for my good.

His Providence is so immense and powerful that although it embraces all of creation, it takes care of every small detail of my life, to the very hairs of my head.

His Providence surrounds me so completely that I neither live nor move without it.

He keeps the entire universe in perfect order for my benefit and pleasure, and yet He seeks His rest and pleasure in my soul.

He takes care of me as if I were the only being He ever created. Every facet of my life is important to Him—nothing is too small for His interest or too great for His Power.

Nothing escapes His Providence for He holds all creation, animate and inanimate, in the palm of His hands, working and arranging all things for the good of my soul.

His Providence extends to the sufferings in my life, even the most painful, for He weighs every sorrow in the scale of His Mercy, fitting to my shoulders the cross I can carry best.

God's providential action is present in every human event — in my life, in my country, in the whole world.

Everything that happens is a message to me of this providential care and interest.

His Providence protects the freedom of His creatures by permitting evil, but it turns that evil to some good for those who love Him.

His providential care reaches to the painful and difficult situations in my life, as incomprehensible as that may seem, and turns them all to my good.

His Providence gives me the opportunity of rising after a fall with deep humility and greater confidence in His strength.

His Providence helps me choose the right thing at the right time but stands by me if I make the wrong choice.

An All-Provident God loves me.

CONSIDERATION

The Father disposes and directs everything for His own honor and glory and for my good. His Providence fixes the order by which I will glorify Him, and as the image of Jesus grows brighter in my soul, that image is reflected back to the Father.

ON GOD, HIS HOME, AND HIS ANGELS

The Father sees Jesus and my soul shares more and more in the life of God. Jesus reminded me of this when He said, "It is to the glory of My Father that you should bear much fruit" (John 15:8). "All I have is Yours (Father), and all You have is Mine, and in them I am glorified" (John 17:10).

Everything that happens in my life is ordained or permitted by His Providence for my good. I may not understand why some things happen, but my contemplation of His Providence assures me that I can trust Him in the darkness and know He looks after me as a mother her only child.

He knows my needs, difficulties, and desires. He listens to my every sigh and sees every tear. His Providence surrounds me completely, and though I do not see the end of the road, I need never fear, "His Providence rises before the dawn."

PRAYER
Wise and Merciful Father, Your Providence surrounds me and directs me with loving concern. Grant me the humility to give myself completely to Your care.

SCRIPTURE
Lord, You are good to all and Your tender mercies are over all Your works. Let all Your works praise You, O

Lord! You open Your hand and fill with blessings every living creature; You execute judgment for them that suffer wrong; and give food to the hungry. You loose them that are fettered, and enlighten the blind. You lift up them that are cast down; You love the just, O Lord. You heal the brokenhearted and bind up their bruises. You cover the heavens with clouds, and prepare rain for the earth. You make grass to grow on the mountains. You give the beasts their food.... O Lord, at the remembrance of Your immense Goodness all creatures break forth in praise and acclaim Your liberality. (Ps. 144-146)

The Mercy of God

The Father showed His Mercy when He sent His Son to bridge the gulf between His Holiness and my misery.

His Love bends down to my weakness and forgives.

He pursues my soul with love and tenderness when I sin by giving me a conscience to discern my offense.

He pardons and cancels all my debts when He sees my sorrow, and hears the sighs of my repentant love.

ON GOD, HIS HOME, AND HIS ANGELS

It is not enough for Him to forgive my sins when I repent — He covers my wounds with the Precious Blood of His own Son and makes my soul beautiful to behold.

He wants me to bury my sins and the burden of my weakness in the ocean of His Mercy so that not a trace of them remains.

I look at the universe — vast and immense — and yet, in my regard, His Mercy is beyond all that — it is Infinite.

I have only to say, "I'm sorry" with sincerity, to bring down upon myself His forgiveness and compassion.

His Mercy is drawn to my misery like a magnet and envelops my soul like a protecting shield.

His Mercy encompasses me to the degree that He no longer remembers my offenses.

When I am repentant, His Mercy toward me glorifies Him to such a degree that all of Heaven rejoices.

No matter how hideous the sin, His Mercy reaches out tenderly to one act of sorrow and contrition.

His Mercy is so great that I will never be able to comprehend its length and breadth.

His Mercy is limited only by my lack of confidence.

He revealed to me His own intimate life by creating me to His image and likeness and then elevating that likeness by giving me a share in His own nature at Baptism.

A Merciful Father loves me.

CONSIDERATION

I am the recipient of God's Mercy, and the best way to show my gratitude for His Mercy in my regard is to be merciful to my neighbor.

I find it hard to forgive and forget, so I must absorb some of His Mercy by bringing to mind how God is the first to reach out to me when I have offended Him. He does not remind me of my sin, nor does He remember my offenses—His Mercy is vast and unending.

He stoops down to me with great compassion and heals my imperfections with His Perfections, my weakness with His Strength, my coldness with His Love, my frustration with His Peace, and my darkness with His Light.

The realization of my own weakness and the contemplation of His Mercy will make me understand the misery and imperfections of others. There is no other Attribute in which

ON GOD, HIS HOME, AND HIS ANGELS

I can participate, that will imprint the image of Jesus on my soul as quickly as Mercy.

When I am merciful, I resemble Jesus, the perfect image of Mercy—and the Father fills my soul with His gifts and graces as I render mercy for mercy.

PRAYER

Merciful Father, let Your Mercy envelop me like a cloak and keep me humble in Your eyes.

SCRIPTURE

O Lord, You are compassionate and merciful, longsuffering and plenteous in Mercy. You will not always be angry, nor will you threaten forever. You have not dealt with me according to my sins nor rewarded me according to my iniquities. For according to the height of Heaven above the earth, Your Mercy surpasses my merits. As a father has compassion on his children, so have you compassion on those who fear You. For You know our frame; You remember that we are dust. Everything will pass; but Your Mercy, O Lord, is from eternity unto eternity to them that fear You. (Ps. 103:8-17, Douay-Rheims)

God Is Love

St. John does not say God possesses love but God *is* love (1 John 4:16). I may *have* love in varying degrees, but with God it is different. To think of God is to think of love; to be filled with love is to be filled with God.

It is difficult for my finite mind to comprehend that what I possess, He is.

When I love someone I wish him everything that is good, enjoyable, pleasant, lasting, and beautiful. The amount of these good things I wish will depend upon the degree of love that inspires these desires. One thing is sure, regardless of degree, love desires to diffuse itself by seeking and procuring the good of others.

God's Love, like Himself, is infinite, and the good He desires for me is infinite — it is beyond my wildest dreams — it is personal and totally mine.

It was an act of God's Love that brought me into existence, and that Infinite Love could not bear to have our nature so different so He infused a part of Himself into my soul at Baptism so that I may call Him Father.

ON GOD, HIS HOME, AND HIS ANGELS

I have a glimpse of Infinite Love when I realize the Father gave His only Son to take upon Himself the humiliation of assuming my human nature, living a laborious life, and dying an ignominious death—just so I could be with Him in the Kingdom.

His Love was not content to call me forth out of nothingness to a natural life—His Love elevated me to a supernatural life—a life of deep union with the Trinity in my soul.

Human love is beautiful and deep but I know of no one who loves like my God, who was willing to sacrifice an only Son for the sake of an enemy.

The Father showed His Love by creating me and sending His Son; the Son showed His Love by living and dying for love of my love; the Spirit showed His Love by coming to earth as Teacher and Guide and making His home in my soul.

Love yearns for equality, but since I could never reach Him, He came down to my level to let me experience the realization of being the sole object of His Love.

Jesus' burning Love for me concealed His Divinity, Majesty, and Splendor to give me courage to approach Him and return love for Love.

Jesus' Love caused Him to leave perfect bliss, unsurpassing joy, and majestic splendor for poverty, privation, and obscurity—for Love of me.

God loves Himself as the only source of Good, and He loves me, not because I am good but because His Love makes me good.

God's Love for me then is free and gratuitous. His Love for me is benevolent because He desires everything that is for my good.

God's Love for me is beneficent because He directs and accomplishes and gives me everything that is for my good.

His Love for me did not begin when I was created. He loved me before time began. Throughout the unnumbered ages of time—before He created a star or a blade of grass, He knew me and loved me.

He never wearies of expressing His Love for me by arranging the innumerable little joys that cross my path.

Throughout His revelations to His Prophets and Apostles He ceaselessly reassures me of His Love and Mercy.

ON GOD, HIS HOME, AND HIS ANGELS

He tries to imprint upon my mind, by images of the Good Shepherd and the Father of the Prodigal Son, His tender Love and Compassion in my regard.

A God of Love, loves me.

CONSIDERATION

All the Attributes of God fill my soul with awe and admiration but none fill it to overflowing as His Infinite Love.

If Love is proven by sacrifice, then He can love me with no greater love for He gave His only Son to live and die for me.

His Love sends me every joy and permits every sorrow. His Love draws me to Himself in consolation, and then withdraws His sensible Presence to purify my soul from all self-seeking.

His Love encompasses me in every difficult situation to assure me that all is well.

I must return love for Love, and render to my neighbor those things I cannot render to God, such as, loving forbearance, loving forgiveness, loving when I am not loved in return.

His Love for me is always infinite — it never changes, it always understands, it constantly reaches out for a return of love, and it blazes forth when I am repentant to assure me of forgiveness. I must make every effort to love my neighbor as He loves me, for in this way I will share more and more in this Divine Attribute.

PRAYER

O Lord, before the world began You knew me and loved me. When the time of my creation arrived You saw me with all my failings and sins and yet You loved me. Let me bury myself in Your Infinite Love like a tiny drop of water in the ocean, that I may be eternally surrounded by Your Merciful Love.

SCRIPTURE

Let us love one another, since love comes from God... because God is Love.

God's Love for us was revealed when He sent into the world His only Son.

God is Love and anyone who lives in love, lives in God, and God lives in him. (1 John 4:9-10, 16)

ON GOD, HIS HOME, AND HIS ANGELS

Omnipotence (Power)

The Power of God is beyond my comprehension. He has merely to will to accomplish.

His Power is so great that He can do anything He wills, when He wills, as He wills, without limitation.

He has only to will before anything exists, and this He does without effort. His Will alone is sufficient for anything to be.

His Power can create the smallest atom or the greatest galaxy—without time, effort, fatigue, or materials. His Will alone is all that is necessary.

God's Word is always effective and always produces whatever it expresses. My words, on the contrary, cannot create anything; I can only change what already is, into something else.

There is nothing impossible to God. His Power can change a sinner into a saint, and derive good from evil, without interfering in the least with man's free will.

His Power is always magnificent and infinite, for the same Power that created Angels—those supreme intelligences, also created the tiny insect without intelligence, and yet both creations are a wonder to behold; each needed His Infinite Power, for each was created out of nothing.

His Power keeps all of His creation in existence without difficulty or confusion. He governs their course without labor or fatigue.

His Power reached out and touched nothingness and all creation came into being.

God alone is omnipotent, for He alone can look at nothing and make something. His Power goes beyond that—it sustains whatever it creates as long as He wills.

His Power never reaches some peak of perfection and then decreases—it is always complete. No matter how much it diffuses itself in creation it never decreases in the least—it is always the same, yesterday, today, and tomorrow.

It was an act of Omnipotence that created my soul. My parents were not allowed even the smallest part in its creation, for my soul has no parts, nor was it made in stages. It was created instantly by God's Power and Will alone.

It took great Power to create such a small image of such a great God, for my soul resembles the Trinity. My *memory* resembles the Father because like Him, I know myself; my *intellect* resembles the Son because I understand what I know; my *will* resembles the Holy Spirit because it has power to choose and to accomplish. I possess then, three faculties, each distinct yet perfectly one. In me, a finite creature, each faculty work-ing with the other makes one soul. In God—Divine Omnipo-tence—each is a Person, Father, Son, and Holy Spirit—one God.

All of creation resembles in some way all three Persons whose Power put it into motion.

There are three kinds of life: *Vegetable* life enjoyed by trees, shrubs, flowers, and fruits; *Sensitive* life possessed by insects and animals; *Intellectual* life held in common by Angels, who are pure spirits, and the soul of man.

God's Omnipotence seemed to make me a composite of all His creation. I enjoy life in common with the *vegetable* world; I share the *animal* life by the possession of my senses; I possess a *rational* life in common with the Angels. I am truly God's exclamation point at the end of His creation.

An Omnipotent God loves me!

CONSIDERATION

This Attribute gives me great confidence and assurance. I real-ize that my Father is so powerful that nothing can oppose His Will, nothing is too difficult.

With a single word He can create, and He is magnificent in all He does. Absolutely nothing is impossible to Him. Everything and everyone I know has limitations—He alone is limitless.

He not only created everything out of nothing but without His sustaining Will all things would go back into the nothingness from which they came.

This realization gives me a feeling of security and stability. Everything and everyone is in His Hands, for without Him the sun would not warm me at noon or the moon give me light at night; fruit would not grow on trees or flowers bloom; water would never quench my thirst or food delight my palate; the smile of a child would never thrill me or the clasp of a neighbor's hand comfort my soul. Verily, His Power constantly works for my good to give me joy and happiness, for all things come to me through Him.

This consideration will be a great help if I am tempted to be proud because I will realize that everything I do I accomplish only because He lets me share His Power. Jesus reminded me of this in His reply when Pilate asked, "Are you refusing to speak to me? Surely you know I have power to release you and I have power to crucify you?" "You would have no power over me," replied Jesus, "if it had not been given you from above" (John 19:10).

Since Scripture reminds me that both my qualifications and authority come from God, I will use them with humility, kindness, and gratitude, knowing I must render an account of my stewardship.

Prayer

O God and Father, You created all things from nothing; You sustain them without effort; You govern them without fatigue; You provide for all from Your abundance which never diminishes; I rest in Your Power knowing You have created me out of Love.

Scripture

In the beginning, God created the heavens and the earth...God said, "Let there be light, and there was light"..."Let there be a vault in the waters to divide the waters in two"... "Let the waters under the heavens come together into a single mass, and let dry land appear"... "Let the earth produce vegetation: seed-bearing plants and fruit trees with their seeds inside"... "Let there be lights in the vault of Heaven to divide day from night"...

Let the waters teem with living creatures, and let the birds fly above the earth within the vault"… "Let the earth produce every kind of living creature, cattle, reptiles, and every kind of wild beast"… "Let us make man in Our own image—in the likeness of Ourselves." (Gen. 1:1-27)

Goodness

God is Good. He is the only Good, not because He possesses Goodness but because His very being is Infinite Goodness.

God communicates to me and my neighbor some of His Goodness. I must always remember this and never envy my neighbor, for every good we possess comes from God.

I draw from this one source of Goodness all the good I desire by ever uniting my will to His.

His Goodness rewards the desires my efforts have not accomplished.

Goodness belongs to God by nature and it cannot be diminished as it diffuses itself to His creatures. He is always infinitely Good.

ON GOD, HIS HOME, AND HIS ANGELS

All the evil in the world and in hell never lessens His Goodness. Though I reject His Love, His Goodness continues to seek me out until death.

His Goodness elevated me, a finite creature, to the heights of Divine Adoption. His Goodness gives me a reward for what His Grace accomplishes through me.

Everything He created is good, and His Goodness is so diffusive that the quantities, qualities, and dimensions of His creation stagger the mind. The variety of fruit, each with its own taste, size, and color; the variety of flowers, rocks, precious stones — everything He created overflows in abundance.

His Goodness gives me music, friendship, love, joy, happiness, success, and all the other good things that cross my path to thrill my soul.

His Goodness saw my misery and sent His Son to redeem me, His Holy Spirit to sanctify me, and His Eucharist to be with me until the end of time.

His Goodness gives me reflections of Himself in the intellect of man, the immensity of the universe, the variety of creatures, and the beauty of the earth.

His Goodness is so magnificent that it draws good out of evil.

A Good God loves me.

CONSIDERATION

It is often difficult for me to be good because I find it hard to love and goodness springs from love. It is the fruit of love and the effect of love. To love is to wish another well—the cause of that desire is love and the effect is Goodness.

Love is an interior disposition and is manifested by Goodness. God's love for me is not dormant but active. He constantly shows me that love in many ways, and my love must respond by an awareness of these manifestations and a humble gratitude.

My love for my neighbor, like God's love for me, must manifest itself by doing all in my power to obtain my neighbor's good.

My love must express itself not only by feeding the poor and visiting the sick, but by a spirit of gentleness in dealing with others, by a joyful attitude, by politeness with young and old alike, and by being thoughtful and concerned with the needs of others.

ON GOD, HIS HOME, AND HIS ANGELS

PRAYER

Good God, penetrate my soul with Your Goodness, that I may radiate Your Love and concern to my neighbor. Give me all the light and strength I need to be a neighbor to everyone, and to do all I can to obtain the good my love desires for them.

SCRIPTURE

I say this to you: love your enemies and pray for those who persecute you: in this way you will be sons of Your Father in Heaven, for He causes His sun to rise on bad men as well as good, and His rain to fall on honest and dishonest men alike. For if you love those who love you, what right have you to claim any credit? Even the tax collectors do as much, do they not? And if you save your greetings for your brothers, are you doing anything exceptional? Even the pagans do as much, do they not? You must therefore be perfect (good) just as your Heavenly Father is perfect (good). (Matt. 5:43-48)

Make no mistake about this, my dear brothers, it is all that is good, everything that is perfect, which is given us from above. (James 1:17)

God Is Immutable (Changeless)

God is Infinite in all His Attributes. There is nothing that can be added to them, and no matter how much He diffuses His perfections to His creatures, they are never diminished. "There is no such thing as alteration, no shadow of a change" (James. 1:17).

His Will is changeless because He wills only what is good for me. Even when I offend Him, His Will always desires my good, His Love reaches out for a response, and His Mercy extends forgiveness.

God is Love and He cannot change. He loves me always, and that Love is Infinite.

God sees everything, past, present and future, as an overall picture ever before Him. He is ever exercising His infinite attributes in His creation—without ever diminishing from or adding to His perfections.

All things are seen in one glance of an Infinite God who never had a beginning and will never have an end. This all embracing, changeless glance is not static but ever active and working with the greatest vitality because it is perfect in all it accomplishes.

ON GOD, HIS HOME, AND HIS ANGELS

His yesterday and tomorrow are all wrapped in a today that knew no beginning and has no end.

God's life subsists by itself and does not depend upon anything outside Itself, for all things derive their life and existence from Him.

His life is not subject to any progression because it is all perfect. There is no succession of knowledge in God for He knows all things and nothing can be added to His knowledge.

In God there is no growth in love for He is Infinite Love. He does not become more merciful as time goes on — He is Mercy itself.

The evil His creatures heap upon themselves and the offenses they give Him do not diminish His Goodness towards them but only make it gush forth like a torrent in the desert.

He does not become provident because of my needs. He is provident before my needs manifest themselves.

His wisdom reaches from end to end in His creation, not only to keep it in order but to keep it in existence.

An Immutable and Eternal God loves me.

CONSIDERATION

I am limited in everything I do and I am in a state of constant change. My mind, body, ideas, likes and dislikes, tastes, and knowledge are all subject to numerous changes during my life. It is difficult for my mind to comprehend in even the smallest degree a Being whose nature is changeless.

The very mystery of the eternal and changeless nature of God gives me a feeling of security and stability.

My weakness and frailty fade into nothingness in the light of the realization that I am the beloved of the Eternal God.

His changeless nature finds its delight in giving me a participation in His Eternity by making my soul immortal, adopting me as a son, and through the merits of Jesus, promising me that I shall rise on the last day.

I can believe and put all my trust in my Immutable Father.

PRAYER

O God, though moment succeeds moment in my life and these are filled with uncertainty and doubt, I find comfort in Your unchanging Love, Mercy, Providence, and Goodness. You are not satisfied that I am the recipient of these

ON GOD, HIS HOME, AND HIS ANGELS

Attributes—You give them to me as my very own, as much as I desire to possess, in this life and for all eternity. Though I change often, give me serenity of soul that I may sail the stormy sea of life anchored to Your Immutable and Eternal Love.

SCRIPTURE

The Lord is the everlasting God who has created the ends of the earth. He shall not faint nor labor, neither is there any searching of His Wisdom. (Isa. 40:28)

No; I, Yahweh, do not change. (Mal. 3:6)

Eons ago, You laid earth's foundation; the heavens are the work of Your hands; all will vanish, though You remain, all wear out like a garment; like clothes that need changing You will change them; but Yourself, You never change, and Your years are unending. (Ps. 102)

Jesus Christ is the same yesterday, today, and forever. (Heb. 13:8)

He has imposed an order on the magnificent works of His Wisdom; He is from everlasting to everlasting. (Eccles. 42:21)

Lasting to eternity, Your Word, Yahweh, is unchanging in the heavens; Your faithfulness lasts from age to age. (Ps. 119:89-90)

Omnipresence, Immanence, and Transcendence

Omnipresence—God is everywhere.
Immanence—God is in everything and in me.
Transcendence—God is above everything.

OMNIPRESENCE

The most consoling attribute of God, next to His Love, is the reality of His Presence everywhere through His Essence, and His Presence in my soul through grace and the Eucharist.

Love demands the companionship of the beloved, and God is with me at all times.

God must sustain everything He creates—He communicates existence to all creation. This being true, He must be present when He operates and so, even in a sinner, God dwells in substance, else the sinner would cease to exist.

To see His Presence in nature, as His Power gives it life and beauty, is to be filled with awe at His Greatness.

My God is not satisfied that I see His Presence everywhere (Omnipresence), He has deigned to come and dwell in my very soul through Grace (Immanence).

IMMANENCE

All of God lives in me—He lives in me in a purely supernatural way—in the deepest recesses of my soul.

This Presence of God goes beyond just sustaining my soul—His Presence in me is a Presence of Love and Friendship.

My soul, in a state of grace, carries God within it. I know Him through Faith, I trust Him through Hope, and I possess Him through Love.

St. Paul tells me that God dwells in me as in a temple. This Presence raises me above my natural level to a supernatural level. It is the gift of all gifts—to have my Creator take up His abode in my soul. The Father lives in me, the Son lives in me, and the Holy Spirit lives in me.

His Power keeps me in existence, but His Indwelling goes beyond that and gives me the opportunity to live in Him and through Him.

Jesus said, "The Kingdom of God is within you" (Luke 17:21)—this means I have only to look within my own soul to find Him.

Jesus promised that if I do His Father's Will, He and the Father will come and manifest Themselves to me (John 14:21).

He offers me His intimate friendship and a life of peace and joy by living within the secret chamber of my soul.

His Presence within my soul is hidden because it is spiritual, and the fruits of that Presence have the power to transform me into a son of God.

The power of this Divine Indwelling can make me into a new person. It can slowly detach me from those faults and things in my life that weigh me down and keep me from reflecting Jesus.

St. Paul explained this beautifully when he said: "... He is not far from any of us, since it is in Him that we live, and move, and exist" (Acts 17:28).

ON GOD, HIS HOME, AND HIS ANGELS

The Presence of God in my soul through Grace places me on the level of a friend in my relationship with God. He is present as Father, as Friend, and as Guest. A deep awareness, through recalling this marvelous truth to mind, will give me all the strength and power necessary to rise above myself and live a more supernatural life—glorifying the Father by bearing fruit through the Son in the power of the Holy Spirit.

I can often go into the sanctuary of my soul, that secret place, and speak to Him as a friend speaks to a friend—Adore Him as Lord and Life-giver, Praise Him as the One who alone is Holy, Thank Him for raising me up from nothingness to a son of God, and make Reparation for my sins by loving repentance. I can do all this in the depths of my soul, alone with God, anytime, anywhere, because He deigns to live in me.

I need not raise my eyes to heaven but only lower them to my heart. I need not raise my voice but only whisper an act of love. I need not look around me to seek Him, but only within me to find Him.

He is "nearer to me than breathing and closer than hands and feet." I am a living temple, in which God dwells, to manifest His perfections to my neighbor. I must often shut out the ramblings of my imagination, the inordinate desires of my senses, and the selfishness of my will, and enter into the interior of my soul where in the darkness is the light of faith, trust is the hope of things to come, and love is the possession of a power that makes me holy.

My soul is like a diamond that the trials and sufferings of life have cut into many facets. The light of God's Grace enters that diamond and reflects that beautiful light for all to behold.

The diamond and the Light are different in nature—one is finite and limited, the other infinite and unlimited. Nevertheless, the diamond and light together shine with such brilliance that they are thought to be all one. To look upon them is to see only light.

So it is that with God's indwelling in my soul, I become by Grace what Jesus is by nature—a son of God.

All the beauty in the world fades away into ugliness in comparison with the magnificence of one degree of Grace—a little bit of God in me.

Jesus lived and died that I may participate in His Father's perfections. His Love and Goodness looked upon my misery before time began and decided that He wanted me with Him in His Heaven forever.

But how to elevate such a creature as I except to give me something I would never dream of or ever begin to merit? He would exert His Omnipotence and become weak, that I might be filled with His Immanence and become great.

He lives in me that I may reflect His very own life and perfections and glorify the Father whose eyes behold Jesus in my soul.

To keep that image clear and more reflective, He gives Himself to me in the Holy Eucharist as food for my soul. I must participate in His nature more and more every day if I am to bring forth the love of Jesus and be a son of the Father.

It is easy to understand a God being everywhere and creating everything by His Power and Wisdom. But it is beyond my comprehension that His Omnipotence did itself violence and became man just to be like me. His Immanence constrained itself in a little Host to be my food. His Infinite Love prepares my soul to be transformed into Him.

Only God could leave me and stay with me at the same time. His physical Presence ascended into heaven but His Immanence gives me His Body and Blood, Soul and Divinity in the Holy Eucharist. Every time I receive this Sacrament, whose power is beyond my comprehension, I receive more of God. The pool of my soul becomes brighter and His Divine reflection more radiant.

He knew my faith would waver at times and I would need something tangible to speak to and gaze upon, so He gave me Himself in a miraculous way in the Holy Eucharist — as Friend when I'm in need, as Companion when I'm lonely, as Strength when I'm weak, as Mercy when I fail, as a source of Joy when I'm sad, as Peace in the midst of turmoil, and as a Power to help me press ahead with confidence for the struggle to come.

He has given me His Presence in Scripture — to guide me along the path of life, to direct me in the right way, to reveal to me His Attributes, His Son and His Spirit, to feed my soul with His Word, to encourage me when things go wrong, to show me His Will, to assure me of His forgiveness, to give me hope when all seems lost, to tell me how much He loves me, and to give me a glimpse of the Kingdom and the Glory to come.

God is present to me in another way, and of all the various ways He is present to me, perhaps this is the most difficult to understand — it is the Presence of God in my neighbor.

ON GOD, HIS HOME, AND HIS ANGELS

It would be easy if everyone I met were Christ-like, but this is not so, and yet, Jesus tells me that whatever I do to my neighbor I do to Him. The Presence of God in my neighbor is so real that He counts as done to Himself the things I do to my neighbor.

I must see His Presence in everyone. In the sinner, He dwells in Essence by the fact that He keeps him in existence. In Christians, He dwells through Grace. I cannot judge how God dwells in my neighbor for I judge only by appearances and God judges the heart.

One thing I must keep in mind—that I should treat my neighbor as I would treat God, because His Presence, either by Essence or by Grace, is Infinite and Holy, and my conduct should be determined by His image in the soul of my neighbor rather than my neighbor's limitations.

TRANSCENDENCE

As I begin to see His Presence around me in nature and the universe, in His Word, in my neighbor, in the Eucharist, and in myself, I must understand that although God is in everything He created—everything He created is not God—He is above it all as Supreme Being.

Only His Son and His Spirit share His nature on an equal basis, and everything and everyone else are reflections of His attributes—created to give Him glory and diffuse His Goodness.

No matter how much I know about God, He transcends all my knowledge of Him. My knowledge of Him will never be comprehensive.

For all eternity I will continue to receive new lights and knowledge about Him that will thrill my soul with awe and wonder.

No matter what my concept of His perfections—His Mercy or Goodness—it all falls short of what He really is; I must use symbols in words, and pictures in images, to describe the transcendence that my mind cannot understand. My intellect will never be satisfied, it will never rest in my knowledge of God, for He transcends all images and words. He is infinite in all His perfections.

My idea of mercy is not His Mercy, because my ideas are of necessity limited, as I am limited. His Mercy is far above any human concept. If I could keep this in mind when I fall, I would never be discouraged or despair.

ON GOD, HIS HOME, AND HIS ANGELS

His Goodness is not my goodness, because my goodness goes just so far. His Goodness is endless, unlimited, pure, and absolute.

God will far transcend everything I know about Him and this will be so for all eternity.

It is an exhilarating thought to realize I will never exhaust the number of His attributes or their infinity. I am called to participate in these perfections in whatever degree I desire. In that eternal now I shall gaze upon Him in wonder, I shall be filled to overflowing with love, and I shall learn new and exciting mysteries, never before known, without ever exhausting the Source from which my beatitude springs.

Unlike earthly heroes, who always fall short of my ideals, God will eternally transcend all I could hope for. If I possessed all the knowledge of God amassed by all the great minds and saints in the world, it would be only a beginning of what remains to be learned.

What makes God, God, is the fact that He is beyond anything I can know about Him, and yet, He reveals Himself to me in a real way, a way in which I can participate in His very nature.

His Power accomplishes the impossible, and His Infinite Transcendence stoops down to me through His Goodness. He dwells in me through His Immanence, and transforms me into Jesus through His Spirit of Love.

> *An All-present, Immanent, and*
> *Transcendent God loves me.*

CONSIDERATION

I must make an effort to become more aware of God's Presence everywhere. I must see Him in all His nature and creation. There are so many vestiges of His Power and Being in everything around me but they will be lost as long as I am blind to their existence and beauty.

I can be so absorbed in my own problems and difficulties that the beauty and peace around me are lost in a maze of imaginary clouds that keep me in a tiny cramped world.

I must look beyond what is visible and see the invisible reality. My life must take on another dimension—a spiritual dimension—the ability to see God and His creation together and not separately.

The Presence of God in my own soul must be the object of my special attention. I must not permit the mystery of this Presence and my inability to understand how He lives in me, prevent me from reaping the fruit of this marvelous Presence. I will humbly turn within my soul to adore, thank, praise and love Him. The Holy Trinity lives in my soul, for the Father living in me continually generates His Son, and from the Father and Son together, proceeds the Holy Spirit. I must be emptied of myself by recalling often during the day, that all of Heaven lives in me.

This Presence in my neighbor will be an aid in treating him as I would treat God, but I will need strength to see God in everyone, and His Presence in the Eucharist will give me more of Jesus so I can be patient, kind, and forbearing.

When I see His Transcendence and the many different ways He is present to me, I realize that only an Infinite Love could have the power to come down to my level, surround me with omnipotence, raise me up and hold me in the arms of His Fatherly care.

PRAYER

Lord and Father, Your Son Jesus gives me tangible proof of Your Presence in my soul by giving Himself to me in the Holy Eucharist. Through the power of Your Spirit's gifts,

*let that Presence bear fruit and give proof to my neighbor
that Jesus is Lord.*

Scripture

Where could I go to escape Your Spirit? Where could
I flee from Your Presence? If I climb the heavens, You
are there, there too, if I be in Sheol.

If I flew to the point of sunrise, or westward across
the sea, Your hand would still be guiding me, Your right
hand holding me. (Ps. 139:7-10)

I shall ask the Father and He will give you another Paraclete
to be with you forever, the Spirit of Truth…you know Him
because He is with you—He is in you.

On that day you will understand that I am in the Father,
and you in Me and I in you (John 14:17-21).

Make your home in Me as I make my home in you. As
a branch cannot bear fruit all by itself but must remain part
of the vine, neither can you unless you remain in Me (John
15:3-5).

ON GOD, HIS HOME, AND HIS ANGELS

> High over all nations, Yahweh!
> His glory transcends the heavens!
> Who is like Yahweh, our God?
> Enthroned so high, He needs to stoop
> to see sky and earth! (Ps. 113:4-6)

We could say much more and still fall short; to put it concisely "He is ALL."

Where shall we find sufficient power to glorify Him, since He is the Great One, above all His works, the awe-inspiring Lord, stupendously great, and wonderful in His Power? (Eccles. 43:27-29).

His Tender Justice

I must keep in mind that God's Justice is tempered with His Mercy. Man's justice is hard and exacting, but this is not so with God.

His Justice demands His Mercy—I am fortunate if man passes judgment on me with mercy, but God is Just because He is merciful and He is merciful because He is Just.

He knows of what I am made; He knows how difficult it is and how many obstacles prevent me from following Him at times; He knows the light and grace I have had and how many talents have been given me; He knows my circumstances and intelligence—and He makes His judgments in the light of perfect truth. He knows me better than I know myself, and His Justice takes all this into account.

St. Francis de Sales made the statement that he would rather be judged by God than by his own devoted mother.

Because my entire life is before Him, His Justice prevents Him from punishing me immediately after a fall. He patiently waits, heaping grace upon grace, reaching out and calling me to a higher life even though my weakness often disappoints Him.

He has given me free will and His Justice must let me decide and choose, even when that choice is not for my good. But the very Justice that gives me the freedom to make a wrong choice is covered with Mercy and brings good out of the evil my weak will may have brought upon me.

ON GOD, HIS HOME, AND HIS ANGELS

It is because God is Just that He is compassionate. He knows me so perfectly His Justice shows compassion when my neighbor, who sees only the exterior, is ready to condemn me. His Justice excuses me, corrects me, and patiently waits until my vacillating will unites itself to Him.

His Justice gives me everything I need to live and to attain my salvation. If life and society have deprived me of those rights and freedoms that are mine, then His Justice will compensate for them in the Kingdom.

Those who have been deprived of sight will see things in the Kingdom that others will never see.

I think of Helen Keller and realize how beautiful His Justice must have been in her regard. Though in this life she was deprived of sight, hearing, and speech, when she arrived in the Kingdom, the first face she saw was God's, the first voice she heard was God's; the first word she spoke with ease and clarity was "God".

As difficult as her life must have been, the sheer ecstatic joy at that moment and all succeeding moments, must have made all the suffering suddenly seem worthwhile.

Jesus assured me of this when He gave me the Beatitudes. The Father's Justice will give the Kingdom to the poor in spirit and the persecuted; the pure in heart and the peacemakers will be called sons of God; the gentle shall inherit the land; those who mourn will be comforted; those who hunger and thirst will be filled; and the merciful will obtain mercy. Verily, His Justice will make all things right.

His Justice will be lenient on those to whom little is given, but it will require much of those to whom much has been given.

I must leave all judgment to Him. I see only the exterior of my neighbor, and although I think my neighbor would be better if he had more light, God knows just how much light he can accept and His Justice metes out to each one according to His All-wise and Loving Will.

God does not demand that the man given one talent produce ten more, though He would be glorified if he did—He is satisfied with the one talent bearing interest.

When I stray from the right path and His Justice calls for correction, it is always done out of love and for love. All that He permits or takes from me, He does only for my good—to prune me, and to show me His love and forgiveness.

Perhaps I can look at the rays of the sun again to obtain some idea of His Justice. The sun's rays have varied effects on everything they touch. It is the reaction of the object touched that creates the effect — the rays remain the same. Those rays harden some materials and soften others; some they solidify and others they melt. The rays remain the same, but how different are the effects.

God does not put one man in hell and another in heaven. His Justice desires that all men are saved, but as His love shines on all men, providing for their needs, directing their course, — each man responds in a different way. Some give love for love, others give thirty, sixty, and a hundredfold return, but there are others who refuse to love anyone except themselves. The constant rays of God's love shine on their souls but their pride rebels against any dependence upon anyone for love, except themselves. They are sufficient unto themselves and reject the warm rays of God's Love and Providence.

Since He has given these souls free will, His Justice demands they be permitted to choose or reject their only source of joy and love. So it is that some are saved and others are not. His love desires all to be saved, but His Justice will not interfere with their free will.

I am fortunate that His Mercy continues to hover over me, ever ready to forgive and forget if only I repent and throw myself in His all-provident arms.

A Tender and Just God loves me.

CONSIDERATION

I will often think about His tender Justice and have confidence in His judgments. He understands me perfectly and I know I can trust Him to reward the good I have accomplished, and temper the corrections that my faults and sins deserve.

In return for His perfect Justice in my regard, I will be careful not to judge my neighbor since I can never be certain of His motives.

The evil actions of others will call forth in my soul, prayers for God's Mercy and Light. I will try to realize that I am capable of every evil and it is only God's Grace that protects me.

I will neither canonize the good nor condemn the bad, but let the Justice and Mercy of my loving Father render to each according to His works.

On God, His Home, and His Angels

Prayer

Holy and Just God, I place myself in Your tender Mercy.
You know me through and through and I rest content with
the knowledge, that when I am judged it will be by You, who
alone are Just, Holy, and Merciful.

Scripture

Offer Him no bribe—He will not accept it,

Do not put your faith in an unvirtuous sacrifice since
the Lord is a judge

Who is no respecter of personages.

He shows no respect of personages to the detriment
of a poor man.

He listens to the plea of the injured party,

He does not ignore the orphan's supplications, nor
the widow's as she pours out her story…. The humble
man's prayer pierces the clouds

…And the Lord will not be slow

…nor will He be dilatory on their behalf

…until He has repaid each as his deeds deserve and
human actions as their *intentions* merit, until He has

judged the case of His people and made them rejoice
in His Mercy.

> Mercy is welcome in time of trouble
> like rain clouds in time of drought. (Eccles. 35:11-24)

Omniscience (God Knows All Things)

God knows all things in a most perfect way. He knows the
thoughts of every angel and human being He ever created or
will create—all in the same moment.

There is no past with God and no future. Everything is
present to Him. He sees it all clearly, fully, and accurately.

At this moment He sees my entire life with all its desires
and ambitions. He knows me as an individual and not as a
part of a huge mass of humanity. He knows me so intimately
that it would be impossible to know me any better—my secret
aspirations are before Him and all those desires never expressed
in words.

He also knows everything I would do under every possible circumstance and in every state in life. There is nothing
that concerns me in any way of which he does not have full
knowledge. His knowledge not only encompasses my actions

in various circumstances, but my very thoughts. He knows me through and through and still He loves me. I wonder if I have any friend who would love me under those conditions.

God's love of me does not depend upon His knowing only my good qualities. His perfect knowledge of me exercises His Mercy and Goodness, and His Love for me is gratuitous. He loves me for myself alone—because He knows my needs so perfectly.

I must bring God's Omniscience to mind when I meditate upon the life of Christ. Every event in the Master's life is present to the Father. If I think of Jesus in the Garden of Olives, and I see Him in great distress of soul, the Father sees that event, as He sees me at this moment.

In the mind of God, His knowledge of that event and my presence now, are in one and the same moment. This being true, I can recall that scene, kneel before Him, and take His Hand in mine, look into His tear filled eyes and tell Him I love Him.

Wonder of wonders! He saw me then as I am now and was comforted by my love.

I must keep this in mind when difficult situations come my way. I can go back and unite my pain and disappointment to His, and know that He was comforted then and is glorified now by my patience and joy in suffering.

It is assuring to realize that God's Infinite Knowledge of all His creation does not interfere with His personal relationship with me.

He knows me as if He knew no other, and this knowledge is not diminished because He knows millions and millions of other people.

I cannot think of more than one thing at a time, and if I try I end up confused and tired. It is an exhilarating thought to know that my God possesses all knowledge to the point that absolutely nothing can be added, and He does this without confusion or fatigue.

An All-knowing God loves me!

CONSIDERATION

I will find joy in the realization that my Father knows everything there is to know. Jesus partook of this Infinite Knowledge, and yet He permitted Himself to be taught the carpenters' trade by one of His creatures. The Holy Spirit partakes of this

ON GOD, HIS HOME, AND HIS ANGELS

Knowledge and yet He stoops to my capacity and gives me only as much as I can hold and render an account of.

This is a wonderful lesson for me. God, who knows all things, is so patient with my small amount of knowledge. He does not expect more than He has given, and He is patient even when that little is not used to capacity.

I must be careful never to make anyone feel inadequate or stupid in my presence, especially if their I.Q. is below my own. Neither must I make gods out of those intellectuals whose knowledge, however great, is only a particle of His.

PRAYER

All knowing Father, give me all the knowledge I need to be more like Jesus. Let Thy Spirit teach me how to be humble, kind, and patient, so that the reflection of Thy Son may grow brighter in my soul.

SCRIPTURE

Yahweh, You examine me and know me,
You know if I am standing or sitting, You read my thoughts from afar,
whether I walk or lie down, You are watching, You know every detail of my conduct.

The word is not even on my tongue,
Yahweh, before You know all about it;
Close behind and close in front You fence me round,
shielding me with Your hand. Such knowledge is beyond
my understanding, a height to which my mind cannot
attain. (Ps. 139:1-6)

He has fathomed the deep and the heart,
and seen into their devious ways;
for the Most High knows all the knowledge there is,
and has observed the signs of the times.
He declares what is past and what will be, and uncov-
ers the traces of hidden things. Not a thought escapes
Him, not a single word is hidden from Him. (Eccles.
42:18-20)

Unity

In order to understand God in the smallest degree, I must
look at Him in parts—I say, God is Love, God is Mercy, God
is Providence, but in reality God is One—He is all of these
things at one and the same time.

ON GOD, HIS HOME, AND HIS ANGELS

When He is Merciful, He is loving, provident, compassionate, and wise.

When He is Provident, He is merciful, loving, wise, and compassionate.

He is One in His Nature though He is Three in Persons. He is One in Essence and there is no one equal to Him.

I am very complex. I am made of a body and a soul. My body has many parts and each is distinct. My head is not my foot and my foot is not my arm.

My soul, though spiritual, is also complex. I have various powers and attributes. Memory, understanding, and will are powers of my soul. Compassion, kindness, and mercy are attributes I possess, but in none of these cases can I ever say, I *am* kindness or mercy, etc. I merely *possess* some degree of these attributes.

It is the same with the powers of my soul: my memory is not my will, and my will is not my understanding. Each is distinct, each exerts its own power, and each influences my life in a different way. None of these is the soul itself but merely faculties of the soul.

I can never say of myself, as I can of God, that I *am* love—No, I possess love. And so it is with the other attributes—compassion, mercy, providence, wisdom, etc.

God in His Infinite Goodness lets me share in His attributes, and the more I resemble Jesus, the more these powers will be mine. They will be my possession, and the source of these powers will always be God, for He lives in me.

Because I am dependent upon God for all good things, I am of necessity complex and composed of many parts, whereas God is absolutely One. He does not possess these attributes—He *is* these attributes. They constitute His very Being. He is not loving—He *is* Love. He is not provident—He *is* Providence. He is not wise—He *is* Wisdom.

These qualities, called attributes, are not in God or of God; they *are* God. His infinite perfections *are* His very substance.

It is difficult for my finite mind to comprehend, but the truth is that His love, justice, mercy, goodness, wisdom, etc., are just different names for His Essence—His Godhead.

God contains in one perfection all the perfections of His Being. All the perfections in every creature ever born are in God as one perfection. He is always the good, loving, beautiful, gracious, and wise Being.

ON GOD, HIS HOME, AND HIS ANGELS

I look at them separately because God affects my life in different ways. When I am in need, He is Provident, when I fall, He is Merciful, when I feel lonely, His Presence comforts me—but it is all one God whose Essence manifests Itself in many different ways to take care of me.

God is One and He shares Himself with me because His Son Jesus merited this privilege by His Life, Death, and Resurrection. He sent His own Spirit to dwell within me to raise me up to a participation in these marvelous attributes.

To be called to share in the very nature of God, through Grace, is truly the gift of all gifts. I can glorify God then by uniting my will to His and manifesting to my neighbor God's Providence, Love, Kindness, Compassion, and Mercy, as He lives in me.

In God there is no difference between what He is and what He does. His Infinite Intellect embraces all truth at one time.

He is utterly Simple and without complications. There can never be any error in God and no succession of thoughts, but only one thought and this thought comprehends everything.

His Will, too, is but one single act—always willing good, and only permitting evil in order to derive a greater good.

Imagine having a million oceans in one place. Though all are made up of tiny drops they form a single ocean. You cannot say the water is separate drops. The difference between this mass of water and God is that as He gives me more and more drops from the ocean of His Attributes He is never diminished. He is always the same but I can grow and grow. I can receive a drop of mercy and compassion, and behold, I also have love and goodness.

I need not be discouraged because the good qualities I possess are imperfect. My joy consists in *His* Perfections, not my own. My happiness lies in gazing at *His* absolute, unchanging perfections and not my ever changing virtues. My Serenity is secure as I contemplate the deep, tranquil ocean of His Immensity.

Litany of the Divine Attributes

Divine Essence, who alone art holy, I bow before Your Being,
Response: Let me share Your Holiness.

Divine Unity and Simplicity, in whom there is no complexity,
Response: Make me simple and sincere.

ON GOD, HIS HOME, AND HIS ANGELS

Divine Eternity, without beginning and without end, giver of immortality,
Response: Let me spend my heaven with You.

Divine Goodness, diffusing Yourself in everyone,
Response: Make me good and kind.

Divine Wisdom, who designed the length and depth of creation,
Response: Make me wise enough to see Your form behind everything.

Divine Power, creating and sustaining all things with an act of Your Will,
Response: Give me strength to accomplish the things You want me to do.

Divine Providence, whose mantle covers every facet of my life with loving care,
Response: Give me perfect trust that I may work for the needs of today without concern for tomorrow.

Divine Knowledge from whom nothing is hidden and nothing is forgotten,

Response: Let me penetrate the mysteries of Your Being that I may share Your Life.

Divine Immanence, who penetrates all things and stoops to live in me,
Response: Let me radiate Your Son and glorify You through the Holy Spirit.

Divine Infinity, which embraces all possible perfections,
Response: Give me a share in Your perfections so that my neighbor may see You in me.

Divine Truth, in whom there is no shadow of deception,
Response: Make me truthful and honest in my dealings with others.

Divine Light, in whom all things are visible,
Response: Enlighten my soul that I may not live in darkness.

Divine Immensity, that fills and contains all things,
Response: Possess me through and through that I may be all things to all men.

ON GOD, HIS HOME, AND HIS ANGELS

Divine Mercy, infinite and without measure,
Response: Let me forgive and forget with love and compassion.

Divine Peace, ever tranquil and serene in the midst of turmoil,
Response: Let me maintain a quiet spirit and be strong enough to accept adversities with peace.

Divine Joy, who alone art the source of all happiness,
Response: Give me that joy that no man can take away from me.

Divine Justice, who judges everything in the light of truth through the eyes of mercy,
Response: Grant that I may not judge my neighbor's motives, but give him the benefit of the doubt.

Divine Immutability, ever the same and never changing,
Response: Make my vacillating will stronger that I may not stray from the path of holiness.

Divine Omnipresence, behind me, before me, and
around me,
Response: Let me see Your Face in everything so that
all Your creation may speak to me of Your beauty.

Divine Compassion, so patient and understanding,
Response: Let me be sympathetic with my neighbor's
needs and give him my love as well as my deeds.

O great God, in whom all perfections are infinite and un-
fathomable, I adore, praise, glorify, and love You. My heart
overflows with joy at the contemplation of Your Beauty and
Splendor. I rejoice that You are so perfect and holy, and I desire
to participate in Your perfections to the degree that will give
You the most glory.

I desire to forget myself by the contemplation of Your Attributes, and I ask that You fill me with these perfections more
and more each day, that I may radiate Your Son through Your
Holy Spirit.

Amen.

HEALING YOUR FAITH
VS. FAITH HEALING

Healing and miracles have been a mystery to men of all times. To some the phenomenon is frightening, while others find it exhilarating. Perhaps it is more often frightening because of the possibility of deception and evil. When God gave Moses power to perform signs, the magicians and diviners of Pharaoh were able to repeat some of those signs.

In pagan times fantastic prodigies were reported during the Hellenistic period and many miracles were performed by Jewish rabbis and the prophets of old. Elias stopped the rain from falling for three and a half years. Elisha called forth bears to consume forty-two children, who mocked him and called him "bald head."

God has always worked wonders through His prophets to increase the faith of His chosen people or to correct their disobedience. However, His Enemy can and has imitated some of those miracles to deceive the faithful. Jesus warned us of this when He said, "False Christs and false prophets will arise and produce signs and portents to deceive the elect, if that were possible. You therefore must be on your guard" (Mark 13:23). Jesus asks us to be cautious but not unbelieving. He was deeply hurt one day when the father of an epileptic demoniac said, " 'If you can do anything, have pity on us and help us.' 'If you can?' retorted Jesus. 'Everything is possible to anyone who has faith.' Immediately the father of the boy cried out, 'I do have faith. Help the little faith I have!' " (Mark 9:23-24). How different was the cry of the leper as he shouted, " 'Sir, if you want to, you can heal me.' Jesus stretched out His hand and said, 'Of course I want to! Be cured!' " (Matt. 8:3).

The difference between these two men was that one wondered if Jesus *could* heal and the other wondered if Jesus *would* heal. The father of the demoniac was looking for anyone to heal his son. He tried the Apostles, but to no avail. To him, Jesus was merely another possibility. The man had no belief that before him stood the Son of God. No wonder Jesus said, "You faithless generation … how much longer must I put up with you" (Mark 9:19). The leper, however, believed Jesus was the Son of God, but his humility made him only *request* that he be healed. It is strange that the one with little faith demanded a healing, while the leper, who really believed Jesus was divine, humbly asked and waited. Faith gave the leper the awareness that humility was in order. Scripture informs us that the leper "bowed low in front of Jesus" (Matt. 8:2) as he made his request.

This act of humility was the spirit Jesus desired before His power reached out and touched those in need. The deeper the faith, the greater the humility. The centurion, who asked Jesus to heal his servant said, "Sir, I am not worthy to have you under my roof. Just give the word and my servant shall be cured" (Matt. 8:8). No wonder Jesus said, "I tell you solemnly, nowhere in Israel have I found faith like this" (Matt. 8:10). This beautiful act of trust and self-abandonment on the part of the centurion touched the Heart of Jesus. This man believed Jesus was the Son of God, One so powerful that an act of His Will could accomplish the miraculous. The man humbly waited, "Just give the word," he said and all would be well.

Jesus was also astounded at the faith of the Canaanite woman. She shouted after Him to the dismay of His Apostles, pleading for the deliverance of her possessed daughter.

ON GOD, HIS HOME, AND HIS ANGELS

At first Jesus "answered her not a word" as He reminded His Apostles that He was sent only to the House of Israel. The woman, however, was undaunted. She knelt at His feet in an attitude of humble supplication. "'Lord,' she said, 'help me.' He replied, 'It is not fair to take the children's food and throw it to the house-dogs.'" By this time any proud person would have walked away, indignant and insulted. Not so, this pagan. She merely accepted her lowly position and answered, "Ah, yes, sir: but even the house-dogs can eat the scraps that fall from their master's table." Then Jesus answered her. "Woman, you have great faith. Let your wish be granted" (Matt. 15:21-28).

Two pagans were able to manifest a humble submission to the Will and Power of Jesus whom they believed to be Divine. In both cases, Jesus held them up as examples of faith. Their need and helplessness no longer permitted them to rely upon their own strength as they humbly waited for His power to make their loved ones whole. Neither one had asked anything for himself, only for others.

The miracles Jesus worked were not so much acts of mercy as signs of His Sonship. They were directed towards increasing the faith of both recipient and onlooker. They were symbolic of the messianic age, the coming of the kingdom and the power of the Spirit. When these ends were not accomplished, Jesus worked no miracles. It was for this reason He worked so few in His home town. The Nazarenes' knowledge of His hidden life in their village blocked their minds to the point where any faith in His Divinity was impossible. Their hearts were so hardened, they tried to capture Him as a madman when His miracles were made known to them. They knew Him only as the carpenter's son and the signs of His Divine Sonship were not acceptable. They did not respect His role as Messiah and Savior. Like the father of the demoniac, they did not believe He could perform miracles, and so they refused to ask if He *would* cure their sick. This stubbornness of heart prevented them from that humble patience that asks and waits upon His Will—a Will that ever seeks the good of those He loves.

Today, we too must realize that Faith asks, humbly waits and then accepts the results without hesitation, without doubts. Faith is the asking, for we acknowledge by our request that Jesus is Lord. However, Hope gives us the assurance that whatever answer we receive—be it yes or no—that reply is in our best interest. It is here that Love accepts with joy whatever God's Will requires of us.

This is the faith admired, praised and expected by Jesus from His chosen people, and certainly from those He has redeemed. The prayer of the Christian is always answered, for his prayer is in faith and that faith gives him the humble detachment so necessary to move the mountains of doubt. He never questions God's love when His answer is "no." The Faith of the Christian sees God's Love in every event of His life. He is not preoccupied with himself or his past. When he sins, he asks forgiveness and knows God's mercy forgives and forgets. Unlike the people before and during the time of Jesus, he does not see sickness and suffering as the result of sin or the Enemy. This concept is Old Testament thinking, not New Testament.

The Apostles were imbued with the punishment concept before Pentecost. But we see a change after Pentecost. Though some sins cause social diseases and other illnesses stem from long-term resentments, we cannot attribute *all* sickness to sin or evil. "To those who love God all things work for their good" (Rom. 8:28).

One day "as Jesus went along, He saw a man who had been blind from birth. His disciples asked Him, 'Rabbi, who sinned, this man or his parents, for him to have been born blind?' 'Neither he nor his parents sinned,' Jesus answered. 'He was born blind so that the works of God might be displayed in him'" (John 9:1-4). Jesus is telling us that no one's sin was the cause of this man's affliction. The Father permitted this man to be born blind through natural causes or some malformation before birth. What appeared as an evil, God saw and said, "Let it be." God saw good both in the blindness and in the healing His Son would one day perform.

To think the Father struck this man blind from birth for the express purpose of providing someone for His Son to heal is a monstrous assumption. The blindness was just as much a sign of God's love as the healing. How much evil passed this man by during his life because of this blindness! Was not this blindness a preparation for his soul to accept Jesus as Lord?

This man did not have any faith. He did not know Jesus, nor had he ever heard of Him. The gospel narrative is very lengthy in its emphasis on this fact. When people asked him how he was healed, he answered them by saying, "The man called Jesus" healed him. They asked where this man was, but Jesus had disappeared. Only after the man was expelled from the synagogue did he encounter Jesus, who had heard of his excommunication and sought him out. Only then was Faith enlivened.

"Do you believe in the Son of Man?" Jesus asked. The former blind man looked puzzled and answered, "Tell me who he is so that I may believe in him." Jesus said, "You are looking at him: he is speaking to you." Now it is that the man receives the most important sight of all—spiritual sight. His physical eyes saw a man, but now he was given the opportunity to see God in that man. His cure had prepared his body to see men, but his soul was raised above that level and he now saw God. "Lord, I believe," he answered Jesus, "and he worshipped Him" (John 9:35-39). The miracle was complete. The purpose of healing had come full circle. The man of no faith was healed so the man of new faith would be a witness to others of the power of Jesus. It is indeed strange that the Pharisees, who saw, ended up blind and the man born blind could see! Which of them suffered from evil? Certainly not the man born blind!

There were others whom Jesus healed who had no faith. The man in the Temple with the withered hand was no doubt planted there to test Jesus. Knowing His compassion, the Pharisees intended to trick Him into healing on the Sabbath. After Jesus confronted them with their hypocrisy, He said to the man "Stretch out your hand," and his hand was healed. Neither the man healed nor those who brought the man had any faith. It does not take much imagination to believe that at least the man healed left with deep Faith in Jesus.

Perhaps the most classic example of healing without Faith was the sick man at the Pool of Bethsaida. The particular incident also gives us two other insights. First, this man was the *only one* healed out of great crowds of people. Second, this man was already sitting at the Pool waiting for healing *five or six years before* Jesus was born! Scripture tells us he had this illness for thirty-eight years. Jesus was probably around thirty-two at this time. No, Jesus did not heal everyone. There were times, Scripture says, when He healed all; other times many, and this particular time — one person was healed. One also wonders about the man Peter and John healed at the Gate Beautiful after Pentecost. How many times did Jesus pass him as He went into the Temple and did not heal him? This man who had been miraculously cured was over forty years old (Acts 4:22). Again, a man much older than Jesus — a man Jesus saw time and time again and did not heal. In fact, there is not one recorded healing during His entire hidden life of thirty years. He was God-Man the moment of His Incarnation—so He had power. He was infinite holiness, so He was compassion personified. Why then did He not heal during these thirty years? It was evidently not the Father's Will or time and since we know God is love, we can assure ourselves that no pain or suffering is wasted. The God-Man, who asked His Apostles to pick up the scraps of bread and fish lest they be wasted, will be even more careful that nothing we suffer for Him and with Him will be lost. Jesus was careful whom He healed because a healthy body is often used to sin and not to glorify God. Perhaps this is why Peter tells us in his Epistle that one who has bodily suffering has broken with sin and is thereby ruled by the Will of God (1 Pet. 4:1).

As soon as Jesus had healed the sick man at the Pool, the man picked up his mat and walked away. Jesus disappeared into the crowd leaving the man without the faintest idea who healed him. Later, Jesus met him in the temple and said, "Now you are well again, be sure not to sin anymore" (John 5:14). Jesus did not say the man's sickness was the result of sin. He only impressed upon him that he had just received a great favor from God, his life had to change—a real conversion was in order. Loss of his soul would be a greater disaster than his previous disease.

In examining the cures Jesus performed in proportion to the number of sick in Israel, the surrounding area and the existing nations at the time of His Life among us, we find He healed a small proportion. Even when He fed the multitude it was only twice and then He was disappointed in their reaction. He sadly looked at the crowd as they followed Him to Capernaum and said, "You are not looking for me because you have seen signs, but because you had all the bread you wanted to eat" (John 6:26).

Jesus wanted His miracles to be signs of His Sonship and the coming of the Spirit. They were destined to *give* and *increase* Faith, not provide a Utopia upon this earth. His followers were to see signs and believe and not see signs for their own selfish purposes. His followers were to grow in Faith by adherence to the Father's Will and by carrying the cross His love placed upon them. They were not to use Him or His Name to advance their physical or material welfare. No wonder He said, "Many will say to me 'Lord, did we not prophesy in your name, cast out demons in your name, work many miracles in your name?' Then I shall tell them to their faces: I have never known you; away from me you evil men!" (Matt. 7:23).

There were other miracles Jesus performed besides the healing of diseases and the deliverance of evil spirits. These too were performed with the same end in view—the *Increase of Faith*. The widow of Naim did not know Jesus, but His compassionate Heart wept for her loss. What an increase of Faith in Jesus as she saw her only son rise! The various miracles on the water, such as calming the storm and walking on the water, were done to increase the faith of His Apostles. He chided them at every incident for their lack of faith or their little faith. Even after the resurrection He was astonished at their incredulity. Yet, these are the men who healed the sick and delivered men of evil spirits.

He wanted His Apostles and His followers never to question that He was truly the Son of God. He wanted them to feel free to ask Him for anything, knowing that He had the power to accomplish the miraculous. But never for a moment did He wish anyone to demand anything from the Father. He gave us His example in the Garden of Olives. He asked for the impossible and accepted the Father's "No" with courage, love and trust.

It is because of the danger of presumption and the temptation to lose Hope that Holy Mother Church does not believe in "Faith Healing." "Faith Healing is an attempt to use Divine power as a natural curative agent that is hindered only by insufficient confidence on the part of the sufferer. A Catholic may not submit himself to faith healing which treats divine power as the automatic servant of calculated acts" (*Catholic Encyclopedia*).

We can humbly pray for what we need, be it physical, material or temporal, knowing that our Father is God and is powerful enough to give us whatever we ask, provided it is for our good. Humility enables us to admit we do not always know in what that good consists.

Faith asks, knowing the Father hears us. Hope waits for His reply. Love accepts that reply with joy.

A prayer that does not contain these three elements is a frustrating, anxious prayer. A negative answer causes guilt and introspection, fear and a feeling of hopelessness. Jesus' insistence on doing the Father's Will as the road to holiness embraces every aspect of our lives. Nothing that happens to us is outside that Will, for that Will is directed by infinite Wisdom, who in turn loves us with an infinite love. In joy and sorrow, sickness and health, poverty or riches, success or failure, the Father's Will is the goal of the Christian's life. Like Jesus, he gives his entire self in humble submission to whatever the Father permits or ordains. He is free and at peace for he lives in the Father's Will and basks in the radiance of His Love. He does not excuse the Father's negative answers by focusing his attention upon himself or others as the cause of God's yes or no reply. God loves and constantly, hourly and moment to moment heals our souls by the power of His Spirit. He does this because He is good and we are sinners in need of His help. He is always providing grace and opportunities to heal our souls so the Spirit can transform them into perfect images of Jesus (2 Cor. 3:18). Sometimes this healing is in sickness, sorrow, pain or tragedy and other times in health, joy, success and consolation. Whatever it is, God is at work. The sick who are not cured after they ask the Father for healing, are loved by God in a special way. He trusts that their faith will not be shaken as they share a splinter of His Son's Cross. They witness to the power of His Spirit as He gives weak men the gifts of Fortitude to endure the Cross. They radiate Hope by their acceptance and their souls grow in the image of Jesus as He lovingly directs their feet to walk in His footsteps.

"Blessed are those who have not seen and yet believe" (John 20:29).

THE ANGELS

Sons of Light

Before We Begin

We live in an age of technology and science that demands proof—and yet, we desire mystery. But when God gives us mystery, we seek to destroy it by gross indifference or childish reasoning.

We take pride in our advances in technology and in the fact that we found the invisible power, called "atomic energy"—energy that can heal, destroy, renew, and rebuild. Yet, we deny Angelic Spirits who are also invisible powers who can destroy, heal and renew.

We take pride in geniuses, sprinkled here and there, and yet deny multitudes of Intelligences that stagger the human mind.

We acknowledge evil in the world and man's inability to cope with it, and yet, we deny evil spirits who harass man in an effort to destroy him.

ON GOD, HIS HOME, AND HIS ANGELS

We realize God is infinite and limitless, and yet, we limit His creative powers to the visible world and its inhabitants. We take pride in the fact that we face reality and tell it like it is, and then we spend thousands of dollars on tranquilizers in an effort to forget reality.

We find anything that concerns the other world below the level of our intelligence, and yet—we watch programs and read books dealing with E.S.P. and occultism.

We watch with great interest as science delves in mental telepathy and mind reading and yet, we consider a mental conversation with God or our Angel as wild imaginings and day dreams.

We are full of contradictions and seem willing to accept anything as long as it is within the realm of our comprehension—and yet, our hearts and minds yearn for the invisible reality that pride puts beyond our reach—the reality that only faith and humility can grasp or comprehend.

How true is the saying that to those who believe, no explanation is necessary, and to those who do not believe, no explanation is possible.

St. Paul told a crowd one day that he was being persecuted because he believed in Angels and the Resurrection—so let us look at these creatures of God that Paul believed in, so that we too may believe (Acts 23:6-11).

The Beginning

Scripture tells us in the Book of Genesis, that in the beginning God created the heavens and the earth.

The earth was a formless void — nothingness. It is difficult to understand nothingness. In our existence everything we see is something; even darkness — that absence of light — is something.

Though it may be difficult, it may nonetheless be necessary to go back to God's timeless existence — Eternity — and see God — Father, Son, and Holy Spirit, ever together, ever alone.

His Infinite Goodness desired to share His happiness with others, not because it would add anything to His happiness but just because He is Goodness itself.

And so — God decided to create beings who were like Himself — pure Spirit.

He merely Willed and they existed — numberless Spirits of varying degrees of intelligences — beings who were finite but far above anything the human mind can understand.

Does Scripture say anything about their creation? The Book of Genesis states that on the first day God said, "Let there be light, and there was light" (Gen. 1:3), and then He divided light from darkness.

Yet, the account puts the creation of the sun and the moon on the fourth day. Can it be that the "light", mentioned on the first day, was these pure spirits? Can it be that the separation of the light from the darkness was the battle in the heavens, a battle that was the consequence of a test they were given?

In the Gospel of St. John, Jesus referred to Himself as Light and to evil as darkness, and then He promised that we too would be sons of light.

> The light will be with you only a little longer now.
> Walk while you have the light, or the dark will overtake you;
> he who walks in the dark does not know where he is going.
> While you still have the light, believe in the light,
> and you will be sons of light. (John 12:35)

What better way to explain His Nature as God than to refer to Himself as Light?

We all understand what it means to have light. We speak of it often and pray for it in our daily lives. Jesus promised His Spirit would teach us all things—He would give us light. We ask for light to make a decision, understand Scripture, or probe a mystery.

We refer to anyone who falls into sin as being in darkness. We speak of others being blind to their faults.

All our lives we unconsciously refer to the Kingdom of God as Light and the Kingdom of Lucifer as darkness.

The name "Lucifer" means Angel of Light, and when he rebelled against the Most High he became the Angel of Darkness—Satan—the Avenger.

It is difficult for our finite minds to understand a nature that is pure spirit and so Jesus very simply refers to Himself as Light.

And these pure spirits created to His image would also be as lights, for each being would be different and the number of these creatures would be beyond the mind to comprehend.

They are beings, finite and yet pure spirits, who can converse with God as spirit to spirit. Their intelligence possesses all that God desires them to possess—without effort. Their knowledge is infused and unhampered by the laborious process of learning inherent to human nature.

ON GOD, HIS HOME, AND HIS ANGELS

Being pure spirits, they are able to travel at the speed of thought, governed by a will that is strong and enlightened. Since their source of knowledge is God, they continually learn new mysteries for their source is limitless.

These pure spirits are intelligent, strong, and enlightened, and yet each spirit is different. Just as human minds differ in intelligence, so the pure spirits—pure intelligences—are different.

Some are filled with love and a knowledge of the mysteries of God and some radiate different facets of the Trinity. Each one, in each class, partakes of the light of God in a different way.

Star differs from star and so spirit differs from spirit. Spirits ever soar towards God, without effort or fatigue. They never tire or feel hungry or are hampered by all the limitations incumbent on human beings.

Every new mystery is learned immediately, in its entirety, without their ever forgetting what is learned.

Nothing material can hurt them or deter them. Their understanding has perfect knowledge of God's Will, so when they will to obey it is with full light.

Why do we find belief in the existence of these blessed spirits so difficult? Is the creation of these spirits too much for our pride?

Are we to believe that between God and ourselves there are no other intelligences—intelligences more like God—created in a more perfect way to His image and likeness?

The Lord of all is so magnificent and munificent in His creation that it is illogical to think that there is not a multitude of degrees of intelligences between ourselves and God. And God has revealed to us through the Scriptures that He has created such creatures.

- They are spirits most like God—spirits whose love and will are totally His,
- Spirits who have never offended Him,
- Spirits whose only joy is their Creator,
- Spirits whose intelligence is beyond our comprehension,
- Spirits who have the power to pulverize a mountain, and the gentleness to protect a child,
- Spirits ever aware that their dazzling beauty is merely a reflection of their Creator,

- ☞ Spirits who care for God's creation and His creatures—care with the love and concern of brothers,
- ☞ Spirits whose humility permits them to stand aside, as
  human beings rise above them, because their Creator
  took on that nature,

but it was not always so, because these spirits had to choose
between their Creator and themselves. They were given much,
and the test consisted in choosing between what they possessed
and God.

It was a matter of acknowledging the source of their being
and the supremacy of the Divine Giver.

Would creatures most like God, fully aware of their gifts,
talents, beauty, and power, bow before their Creator as Lord?
Or would they become infatuated with themselves and refuse
to serve, refuse to adore, refuse to obey?

Spirits of such a superior nature would have to have a test
equal to their nature. "To whom much is given, much is re-
quired" (Luke 12:48), and the test would be one in which they
would have to choose between themselves and God—pride
versus humility—truth versus lies.

The Battle

In the Book of Daniel we learn that Daniel received a vision of the great conflict among the Angels (Dan. 10:1). And in the Book of Revelation, St. John gives us some idea of what this battle was and its results (Rev. 12:7).

Each Angel that God created was in himself a masterpiece. Each one possessed his own degree of intelligence and his own beauty.

God would pour out knowledge to those who had the greatest capacity for learning, and they in turn would share their information with others.

It must ever be so, for God has created both spirits and men as social beings — beings who, like their Creator, wish to share their talents, gifts, and knowledge.

Goodness diffuses itself, and the angels, like men, were created by God — good.

Because their nature was pure spirit they understood God and His perfections more clearly than man, and though they did not see Him Face to Face until the test was over, they did not strain their minds to grasp every mystery or to understand the existence of God as man does.

ON GOD, HIS HOME, AND HIS ANGELS

In whatever place they were, God gave them full knowledge of Himself, of His creation, and of other beings — beings inferior to themselves but also made to His image and likeness.

These human beings were a composite of all His creation, possessing a little of every kind of life within them — vegetable, mineral, and animal, and, like the angels, spiritual.

The Angels observed that these human beings were of a nature rather inferior to themselves — their mode of travel slow, their ability to comprehend, difficult.

It would take these creatures years to mature and years to acquire knowledge. They would have times and seasons that changed their surroundings and themselves.

Everything in their creation would pass, and finally, they themselves would die; their souls would leave their bodies, and only then would they come anywhere near to resembling the Angels.

Their sense of sight would be capable of seeing only short distances and small areas.

Their method of expressing their thoughts and ideas would be limited to sounds and symbols.

Their mode of travel would be slow, and only after centuries of experience and knowledge would they begin to travel at any speed.

Their mental faculties were limited and their undisciplined emotions would govern their actions more often than their wills, and it would take centuries of combined knowledge to learn what the least of these angelic spirits knew at his creation.

How different the human nature would be from the angelic nature. It was, at its best, limited, slow, gross and coarse. Yes, these pure spirits were superior in every way to human beings.

Each Angel realized his own perfections and acknowledged that these perfections came from God. An intelligence such as his must admit this truth.

From the first moment of their creation, the angels possessed infused knowledge, given to them without any effort on their part. This knowledge was complete and entire from the first moment it was received.

They were created mature and immortal intelligences, unhampered by age, time, or seasons.

Their mode of travel and communication was as swift as a thought can travel, and without fatigue.

By a mere act of their will they could converse with any other spirit, and that spirit would understand the entire thought without error, misunderstanding, or confusion.

Everything around them was permanent and everlasting and their spirits were ever young and vibrant.

What kind of test would these exalted creatures be given? We can only surmise the nature of this test from the twelfth Chapter of Revelation.

There is enough written in this Chapter to enable us to piece together the mystery of this test.

To God, all things are present; there is no past or future to Him—it is all NOW. Before He created man or angel, He knew the consequences that would follow—He knew that when man offended God, only God could make suitable reparation.

Man's inferior nature would glorify God's Mercy for all eternity.

But before God announced His future plans it would seem that some of the angels must have begun to weaken.

The sin of pride is a gradual thing—a slow process of deterioration that is hardly noticed until it is too late.

Perhaps some of the Angels began to look at themselves and concentrate on their own beauty and grace, so much so that they slowly began to spend more time thinking of themselves than of God. They may have begun to attribute their knowledge to their own ability and talents, oblivious of God's gifts to them.

And then came the staggering proclamation from the Most High: the Second Person of the Most Holy Trinity would become man — Incarnate Word.

Man! For a moment there must have been silence and shock. God made man! Man was so inferior to the nature of a spirit. God would become Man, and, as the God-Man, would be their superior — their Lord and their King!

But this was not all of the test: the God-Man would have a Mother — a Woman — and she too would be raised above them!

Like a flash of lightning, Lucifer, the greatest of all Angels, the one most like the Most High, the one called "Angel of Light" — cried out with a voice of thunder "I will not serve!" Other Angels, of every class and degree of intelligence, all cried out together, "We will not serve."

And then began the battle between pride and humility. Michael rose above all the others and thundered, "Who is like God!"

ON GOD, HIS HOME, AND HIS ANGELS

The battle they fought was not one of swords—swords that make one bleed and die. No, it was a more deadly battle—a battle of intellects, of wills, of ideas and loyalties.

Yes, the result of such a battle is irrevocable—for whichever side a spirit would choose it would be an eternal decision.

He knew only too well the consequences of his choice. If he chose God, he would be in God's Presence forever; if he chose himself, separated from the only source of Goodness and Light, then he would be in darkness, wrapped in his own misery, forever.

Each Angel would have full light as to the test and its consequences.

Then they began to fight for their own opinions, their own rights, and their own loyalties—each making a choice that would set his *will* forever.

As the debate raged on, Lucifer became more adamant. It was not fair for the Word to take on human nature and continue being Lord. Human nature was gross and inferior, and the Most High had no right to make such an unjust decree.

If the Word became man, then all mankind would have the opportunity to become sons of God. Was not the angelic nature, as pure spirit, most like God? Was not he, Lucifer, the greatest of all angels? Was not his intellect superior to them all?

Yes, he, Lucifer, would be Lord and King of Angels and Men. He was superior to them all.

He would not bow before an Incarnate Word; neither would he accept a Woman, the Mother of the Incarnate Word, as Queen of Heaven.

The blow of all blows would be the fact that since the Word would become flesh, all mankind would have the opportunity to arrive at great heights of sanctity—heights above some of the Angels themselves. Yes, they would become brothers because they would share the same Father.

Lucifer and his cohorts would not accept such a humiliation. It was unjust! They were the fruits of the first hour of God's creative powers. They would not share these fruits with those who came at the eleventh hour!

Then Michael rose to the defense of God: God alone is Holy, he reasoned; God alone is Lord; God alone is Most High, He can do as He pleases. Was Lucifer jealous because God chose to be beneficent to those who came last—those whose intellects were below the angelic nature.

Was it not more important that God be glorified than that they as pure spirits be glorified? Was it not God's privilege to give as He willed, since all Goodness came from Him alone?

They were all brought out of nothingness and they owed God eternal thanksgiving for the least amount of grace and glory.

No, it was not a humiliation—it was a truth and to those who cling to truth there would be no humiliation. Would it not magnify the Mercy of the Lord to raise up human beings to the dignity of sons of God by allowing His own Son to become one of them?

Yes, it was just, holy, and right that the Eternal Word become flesh, born of a woman, that other creatures might become brothers.

Lucifer replied with more arguments against this decree: he was the spirit most like God and he would be Lord of men and angels.

As the battle raged, Angels from the different choirs began to take sides—some agreed with Michael, others, with Lucifer.

Lucifer's arguments were very convincing and he "dragged a third of the stars from the heavens" with him (Rev. 12:4).

The longer the battle went on, the more entrenched each side became, until finally Lucifer said, "I will not serve. I will set my throne above the Most High" (Isa. 14:13).

At that final blasphemy Michael cried out, "Who is like God! Victory and power and empire forever have been won by our God and all authority for His Christ" (Rev. 12:10).

Jesus Himself tells us what happened next, for one day when the Apostles became inflated with their own powers, it brought back to His memory the scene that ended the battle in heaven. He looked at them and said, "I watched Satan fall like lightning from Heaven" (Luke 10:18).

Yes, the Angel of Light became Satan—the Angel of Darkness. His pride was a lie, and the Son of God was one day to tell those who followed Satan: "The devil is your father, and you prefer to do what your father wants. He was a murderer from the start; he was never grounded in truth; there is no truth in him at all; when he lies he is drawing from his own store because he is a liar, and the father of lies" (John 8:44).

Pride was born and hell came into existence when these spirits set their wills against God forever. They would always be on fire with jealousy, anger, hatred, and pride. And that fire would reach out to burn others with its sparks of hatred—forever burning with what they considered an injustice on the part of God.

The one thing Lucifer desired was to be the leader—and so he was—leader of demons, father of lies, and prince of this world.

But there was one other thing he desired too, for Scripture says, "As soon as the devil found himself thrown down to the earth, he sprang in pursuit of the woman, the mother of the male child. … Then the dragon was enraged with the Woman and went away to make war on the rest of her children, that is, all who obey God's Commandments and bear witness for Jesus" (Rev. 12:13, 17).

However, Michael and all the other spirits who rallied to the cause of truth and the glory of the Most High, entered into the Beatific Vision. They saw the One they fought for with such courage, for their wills were forever set on God—forever happy, forever at peace.

They all sang together, "Holy, Holy, Holy is the Lord God, the Almighty: He was, He is, and He is to come" (Rev. 4:8).

"Now the persecutor who accused our brothers day and night before our God has been brought down. Let the heavens rejoice and all who live there" (Rev. 12:10, 12).

How art thou fallen from Heaven, O Lucifer, who didst rise in the morning? How art thou fallen to the earth, that didst wound the nations?

And thou saidst in thy heart: I will ascend into heaven, I will exalt my throne above the stars of God, I will sit in the mountain of the covenant in the sides of the north.

I will ascend above the height of the clouds, I will be like the Most High.

But yet thou shalt be brought down to hell, into the depth of the pit. (Isa. 14:12-15, Douay-Rheims)

Friends and Companions

From the moment of his fall, the Angel of Darkness stalked the earth looking for the Son and the Woman.

He must have thought he had conquered when he successfully instilled pride and rebellion into Adam and Eve. What was his surprise when God had mercy on them, and once again he was reminded of the Woman and her seed.

His hatred for God forced him to seek the destruction of all the souls destined to enjoy the glory of Heaven that he had lost.

ON GOD, HIS HOME, AND HIS ANGELS

When, after centuries, he was finally deceived and mankind was redeemed by the life, death, and resurrection of Jesus, his fury was even greater. If he could not drag them all into the abyss, at least he could, by temptation, avarice, lust, pride, and gluttony, decrease their merit and eternal glory.

Though he fell, he still retained his high degree of intelligence and all the powers that were natural to his nature. So he would tempt, deceive and harass mankind and thus deprive God of glory for all eternity.

We are warned in the Epistle of St. Jude never to forget his superior intelligence or his dignity as a spirit. St. Jude speaks of this dignity in regard to both good and evil angels when he warns the people not to use abusive language. He says, "In their delusions they not only defile their own bodies and disregard authority, but abuse the glorious angels as well. Not even the Archangel Michael, when he was engaged in argument with the devil about the corpse of Moses, dared to denounce him in language of abuse; all he said was 'Let the Lord correct you'" (Jude 8-9).

Yes, we must be careful of creatures superior to ourselves in every intellectual way—creatures that are powerful and clever—creatures bent upon our ruin.

God, in His Infinite Goodness, would not pair us up in an uneven battle. No, it would be like a child debating with Einstein.

In His Infinite Mercy and Justice, God would be obliged to give each one of us an angel—an angel who would be equal in every way to the spirit of evil ever working for our defeat.

This Angel would have to be our very own because, as St. Peter said in his Epistle, "the devil goes around like a roaring lion seeking someone to devour" (1 Pet. 5:8). Yes, we would need one of the glorious spirits to fight many an invisible battle for the possession of our souls—battles that are as real as the air we breathe and just as invisible.

Did Jesus reveal these guardians to us? We know that one day He told His Disciples that unless they became as little children they would not enter the Kingdom of Heaven. In other words, they must possess the simplicity and candor of a child to belong to Him (Luke 18:17).

In fact, He said that unless they did possess these qualities they would not enter the Kingdom at all.

With this in mind, He continued His discourse by saying, "See that you never despise any of these little ones, for I tell you that their Angels in Heaven are continually in the Presence of My Father in Heaven" (Matt. 18:10).

We must be careful that we do not take this text of Scripture out of context and imagine some little child of four on the edge of a precipice with a nine-foot Angel pulling him back.

The Master addressed these words to big, strong fishermen, who had, over the years, acquired worldly ways, proud intellects and stubborn wills.

He would have them know that men such as these did not enter the Kingdom.

They were to become trusting and simple children of a loving Father. To impress this upon them He often addressed them as children. He told them

- that they were like children sitting in the Market Place,
- that the good seed was the Children of the Kingdom,
- that the cockle was the children of the wicked one,
- that He would have gathered together His children as a hen gathers her chicks,
- that the children of this world were wiser than the children of light,
- and that they were children of the Resurrection.

Yes, He would thank His Father for hiding the mysteries of the Kingdom from the learned and clever and revealing them to mere children (Luke 10:21).

For all those who belong to the Kingdom of Light were to be humble, simple, and loving children; while those who belong to the Kingdom of Darkness were proud, sophisticated and arrogant.

At the Last Supper discourse Jesus addressed His Apostles as "My little children." Yes, we are all His children and we all need a special angel to protect us from the snares of these evil spirits. God would not deny us this help and protection (John 13:33).

St. Paul reminds us in the Epistle to the Ephesians that "it is not against human enemies that we have to struggle, but against the Sovereignties and the Powers who originate the darkness in this world, the spiritual army of evil in the heavens" (Eph. 6:12-13).

It is difficult enough to face a visible foe stronger than yourself, but how could we resist an invisible foe whose spiritual faculties are so much keener than our own?

We would need someone of equal intelligence, strength, and power as a friend and companion. The Sacred Writer of the Epistle expressed it beautifully when he explained how infinitely superior was the Son of God to any angel, but in the same passage he expresses the angel's role. He says, "The truth is that they are all spirits whose work is service, sent to help those who will be the heirs of salvation" (Heb. 1:14).

Did the first Christians believe in guardian angels? Apparently they did, because it is written in the Acts of the Apostles that when Peter was freed from prison and stood at the door of John Mark's house pounding to get in, a woman, named Rhoda, saw him and told the disciples that Peter was at the door. The disciples thought he was still in prison, and replied, "You are out of your mind. It must be his angel" (Acts 12:12-16).

Although this statement indicates they believed guardian angels were a kind of spiritual 'double' of their charges, we must remember that this was a popular belief at the time.

God's revelations are given and understood slowly. Regardless of how they thought these angels looked, they did believe in their existence and their service to God's people.

The Angel of Darkness must have known of this angelic office too, or else why did he tempt the Master in the desert by saying, "If you are the Son of God, throw Yourself down, for Scripture says:

He will put You in His angels' charge, and they will support You on their hands in case you hurt Your foot against a stone. (Matt. 4:6)

Yes, the belief in spirits, often referred to as angels, was very strong during the time of Christ and after His Resurrection.

So much so that St. Paul in his Epistle had to reprove the Colossians and make them realize the angels' place in creation.

He told them that in Christ was the fullness of Divinity and that we too would find our fulfillment in Him — in Him who is the head of every Sovereignty and Power (Col. 2:9-10).

As Christians, we are a part of Christ's body. We have been given a participation in the Divine Nature, and because of this, we are called to be higher than the highest Angel.

It is no wonder Satan hated these human beings, so inferior in nature but called to be superior by grace.

Yes, Paul would remind us that these glorious spirits did exist — they were fellow servants but that's all.

When Christ did away with our debt by nailing it to the Cross, then the power of the angels, who were guardians of the Law, was ended. They acknowledged His Sovereignty as Lord and Redeemer (Col. 2:14).

The new law of love and grace began and they became our brothers, friends, companions, and fellow servants.

The Angel of the Lord and Angels

It must be remembered that as often as Scripture mentions Angels as distinct beings and pure spirits, it refers also to God Himself as an Angel. This was particularly true when the Lord God appeared to man and gave him some message.

Since the nature of an Angel is pure spirit, man has come to call him 'Angel' because the word means 'messenger.'

Since both God and His created spirits often gave messages to man, they were both simply referred to as an "Angel of the Lord."

We must make a distinction between the two so that we do not fall into the error of mistaking one for the other or of denying the existence of Angels.

In the Book of Genesis when Sarai became jealous of Hagar because she had conceived by Abraham, Hagar ran away. It says that an angel of the Lord stopped her and asked where she was going. When she replied she was running away, the angel said, "Go back to your mistress and submit to her.

I will make your descendants too numerous to be counted" (Gen. 16:9).

Scripture continues to describe the child she has conceived and then says, "Hagar gave a name to Yahweh who had spoken to her: 'You are El Roi' she said, 'Surely this is a place where I, in my turn, have seen the One who sees me" (Gen. 16:7-13).

In still another place in Genesis, when Abraham was about to sacrifice his son, Scripture says, "the Angel of Yahweh called to him from heaven: 'Abraham, Abraham, do not raise your hand against the boy. Do not harm him, for now I know you fear God. You have not refused me your son, your only son. I swear by My own self—it is Yahweh who speaks—because you have done this, because you have not refused Me your son, I will shower blessings on you, I will make your descendants as many as the stars of heaven'"(Gen. 22:11-18).

In the Third Chapter of Exodus, Scripture says an Angel of the Lord appeared to Moses in the shape of a flame of fire, coming from the middle of a bush. As Moses went near, a Voice from the bush exclaimed, "I am the God of your fathers, the God of Abraham" (3:6).

It is evident in these texts that the Sacred Author is describing the appearance of God Himself—His Spirit in a visible form — giving messages of comfort and foretelling future events.

But there are many other texts in Scripture that describe spirits — created spirits — who were also sent by God to give comfort to foretell future events, and sometimes to avenge His enemies.

There is one striking example of one of these created spirits being sent by God to protect His people. "I Myself will send an Angel before you to guard you as you go and to bring you to the place that I have prepared. Give him reverence and listen to all that he says. Offer him no defiance; he would not pardon such a fault, for My Name is in him."(The Angel was God's ambassador.) "If you listen carefully to his voice and do all that I say, I shall be enemy to your enemies, foe to your foes. My Angel will go before you and lead you to where the Amonites are..." (Exod. 23:20-24).

There are many other texts in Scripture that describe one particular Angel, called by St. Paul "the Destroyer." "You must never complain: as some of them did, and they were killed by the Destroyer" (1 Cor. 10:10). "It was by faith that he kept the Passover and sprinkled the blood to prevent the Destroyer from touching any of the first-born sons of Israel" (Heb. 11:27-28).

This created spirit was sent by God to execute punishment upon His enemies and to assist His people in their demands for freedom.

And then there were other spirits sent by God to foretell future events such as the one sent to Daniel to explain the duration of their persecution and future liberation (Dan. 10).

The Angel who appeared to Zechariah, as given in the First Chapter of St. Luke, foretold the birth of John the Baptist.

In the Tenth Chapter of Daniel we find an account of Angels who had charge over nations — guardians of nations.

Then there was the Angel sent by the Father to comfort His Son in the Garden of Agony to give Him strength (Luke 22:43).

Accounts such as these are too numerous to count, but we can be sure that He has revealed the existence of pure spirits, their names, ranks, and the various services they perform, that we may take comfort from their love and protection.

Guardians of Nations

In the Book of Tobias we read that the Angel Raphael refers to himself as one of the Seven who stand in God's Presence (12:15).

ON GOD, HIS HOME, AND HIS ANGELS

The Book of Revelation mentions the Seven Angels who stand in God's Presence (8:2). It states that "in front of the throne there were seven flaming lamps burning, the seven Spirits of God" (4:5).

There are numerous Scripture passages that mention these Seven Spirits standing in God's Presence.

These may be special Angels who perhaps fought more valiantly during the battle in Heaven, or the number seven may indicate all the Angels.

The Angels are all united to God, each in his own special way, and so it can be said they are never out of His Presence.

It is so with all of us. When our thoughts are with God, then we too are in His Presence. Each one of us is in that Presence in varying degrees, and so it could perhaps be said that these Angels, referred to as among the Seven, have a greater capacity for love, and God has filled that capacity to the full.

The names of three of these Seven are mentioned in Scripture, and each one seems to possess a particular gift and mission from God.

Michael is referred to as the Prince of the Heavenly Hosts. His mission as Defender and Protector is mentioned in four different accounts of Scripture.

Gabriel is the Angel who appeared to Daniel, Zechariah, and Mary. He was a Proclaimer, an Announcer of Good News.

Raphael is mentioned in the Book of Tobias, and the whole Book manifests his role as Intercessor and Healer.

Whatever their roles in salvation history, we must remember that the Angels received their power and gifts from God. When we acknowledge their existence, their presence, their gifts, and their concern, we praise God for His Goodness and Omnipotence. How Good is God to let His creatures share His Perfections.

We will look at all three of these special Angels that we may praise God.

One of the key texts on the resurrection of the body in the Old Testament is given in the Book of Daniel, and it is here we learn that Michael is "the great Prince," and that he is the Guardian Angel of the People of God (Dan. 12:1). He is the one whom God promised to Moses when He said, "I will send my Angel before you to guard you as you go and to bring you to the place I have prepared" (Exod. 23:20).

God, in His Infinite Goodness, has not only given each one of us an Angel to guard us, but He has also given nations their own Angel to intercede for their welfare before the throne of God.

And so it was that "In the third year of Cyrus, King of Persia" (Dan. 10:1), Daniel was to receive from God a prophecy of the future of the Kings of Persia, Alexander the Great, and the conflicts of the Seleucids and Ptolemies.

The Angel Gabriel was sent to Daniel for this purpose, but apparently the Angel Guardians of these nations tried to restrain him, not in opposition to God's Will but to give their charges more time to repent.

For Gabriel said to Daniel, "The Prince of the Kingdom of Persia has been resisting me for twenty-one days, but Michael, one of the leading princes, came to my assistance. I have left him confronting the Kings of Persia and have come to tell you what will happen to your people in the days to come" (Dan. 10:13-14).

As Israel had its guardian angel, so these pagan nations had their angels. When Gabriel was sent by God to reveal to Daniel the fate of these pagan nations, their particular Angels began what Gabriel described as "resistance."

Though each Angel is completely united to God's Will, they nonetheless were given charge over these pagan people, and since the future of these people was not known to them, unless God revealed it, they tried to use whatever means they could to help them.

Thus Gabriel tells Daniel that the guardian of the Persians held him back twenty-one days, trying to intercept the message Gabriel had to give — a message that might have contained an unfavorable decree against the Persians.

This may seem strange to us but we must keep in mind that the charge the Angels received to guard these nations came from God, and each Angel decided to convert his nation or at least obtain time for them from the Most High — time to seek the one true God.

The Angels' resistance was one of love and zeal: love for other fellow servants and zeal for the glory of God.

Jesus Himself gave us an example of persevering prayer when He told us to ask but not be satisfied with asking; to seek but not be satisfied with seeking; to knock — and then it would be opened; and so it was with the importunate widow who kept asking for justice.

Likewise, these Angels, ever seeking God's Will, sought every means to assist their charges.

ON GOD, HIS HOME, AND HIS ANGELS

We have an example of this type of resistance in Peter and Paul. Both were Apostles, both filled with the Holy Spirit, both given missions to God's People — the one to the Jews, the other to the Gentiles. Both were given powers to heal, to deliver, and to raise the dead.

Yet, both disagreed violently over circumcision. They disagreed until it was made known to them by God what His Will was in this matter.

We saw Abraham, too, arguing with God, trying to save Sodom and Gomorrah. He asked if these cities might not be saved if he found sixty just men. Realizing this was impossible, he continued to bargain, but not one just man could be found.

And so it was with the Angels: each had power, each had a mission, each sought God's Will, but until that Will was made known, each would work for the welfare of their particular people. As each Angel's knowledge and light is different from another Angel's, it is evident that each would continue to work until they received light as to God's Will and the will of the people they guarded.

Yes, the fate of the nations was a secret, awaiting God's revelation, and for the time being this revelation was hidden from the Angels.

Gabriel tells Daniel that he received the assistance of Michael, one of the leading Princes whom he left to confront the Angels of the Kings of Persia (Dan. 10:13).

Michael was an Angel of higher rank, who continued the struggle with the Angels as they defended the cause of their nations before the Most High.

Apocalyptic writers represented the events of history as if they were decided before they happened on earth. This may be why Gabriel said to Daniel, when speaking of Michael: "I have left him confronting the Kings of Persia" (Dan. 10:13).

This was a dramatic scene in which Daniel sees the opposition of the pagan nations to the people of God, and God's control of all nations.

Daniel prostrated himself on the ground in fear and trembling; his strength left him and his breath seemed to fail.

The Angel told him not to be afraid and Daniel suddenly felt his strength return. And then Gabriel said, "Do you know why I have come to you? It is to tell you what is written in the Book of Truth" (Dan. 10:20a, 21a).

What is meant by this Book of Truth? Since all things are present to God—meaning there is no past or future to Him—He knew the hearts of these pagan people; He knew that no matter how often He reached out to help them they would not turn to Him. He also knew what would happen to these nations if they did not turn from their evil ways.

The fate of these nations was being debated before the Most High as each Angel interceded for his charges, without either one having foreknowledge of the future.

Then Gabriel continues, "I must go back to fight against the Prince of Persia: when I have done with him, the Prince of Javan will come next. In all this there is no one to lend me support except Michael, your Prince, on whom I rely to give me support and reinforce me" (Dan. 10:20b, 21b; 11:1).

This seems to intimate that there are Angels whose missions from God are Guardians of Nations. We can see throughout Scripture, as we have seen with Michael, Gabriel, and Raphael, that different Angels out of every rank are given definite missions from which they never swerved. As they observed the actions and wills of the people in their charge, they began to intercede with God on their behalf; debates arose as to the knowledge, light, and opportunities given to these people and their responsibility before God.

God alone would know the final choice these nations would make, but the Angels would plead for them until the last moment.

Though man's Will and a nation's Will are strong enough to resist God's Will, the Angels would intercede to the end—until that final choice between God and themselves arrived—the choice that would seal their fate forever.

To Gabriel alone God gave the revelation of that final choice and he was sent to Daniel to reveal its contents.

It is important for us to understand that although the Angels are with God they are concerned with their fellow servants on earth—concerned enough to pray, protect, enlighten, and rejoice when they repent.

Prince of the Heavenly Hosts

We have learned from Scripture that it was Michael who fought with Lucifer during the battle in Heaven (Rev. 12).

It was Michael who was appointed Guardian of the People of God during the Exodus (Exod. 23:20).

It was Michael who went to the assistance of Gabriel when he was sent to Daniel (Dan. 10:13).

It was Michael who argued with the devil over the body of Moses (Jude 9).

It is then Michael who is the Guardian of the Church. We can see this role in the Twelfth Chapter of Revelation.

As Guardian of the People of God, and as Defender of the Rights of God, it is logical to think that his protection would continue, as the Church his Lord founded was tempted from every side and weakened from those within and those without.

This champion of the Incarnation continues to defend God's People as they struggle against the forces of evil in the world around them.

He is ever thundering his battle cry, "Who is like God?" He watches the Church throughout the world, ever seeking to uphold the purity of its beliefs and the zeal of its members.

He fought for the rights of God as He decided to become Man. What must have been both his joy and his reward when that blessed day arrived—the day the Christ was born!

When Christ became man, Scripture says, He was like us in all things except sin. Can it be that as *Man* He, too, had a special Angel?

Why would Satan have tempted Jesus to throw Himself down from the pinnacle had he not known the Christ was protected in some special way?

Yes, if Jesus, too, had a special Angel, it would certainly have been Michael—that great Defender of Truth.

Since Michael was appointed Guardian of the Israelites, from whom the Incarnate Word would come, we may speculate if perhaps he was also the Angel who stood with a flaming sword at the gates of paradise after Adam and Eve were expelled.

Was he the Angel who prevented Balaam from cursing the Israelites under his charge?

Was he the Angel who also slew the great army of Sennacherib which was encamped before the Holy City, as Isaiah pleaded with God for deliverance?

Yes, it is written that in one night the Angel of God went out and slew a hundred and eighty-five thousand men.

God had appointed a mighty warrior to guard His People. Who else would slay its enemies but he who guarded them? This champion of truth and justice would ever seek the right of God to do as He pleases. He would protect the people out of whom would come the Christ and the Woman. He would protect the ministers of truth as they spoke God's Word. He would fight against the errors instilled in proud hearts. His armies would combat the demon hosts as they tempted men to deny the rights and sovereignty of their Lord.

Michael would ever have but one goal: to defend the honor and glory of God, the sovereignty of Jesus as Lord, the prerogatives of the Woman, and the welfare of the Church.

Oh, Michael, great champion and defender of truth, protect us from pride, the enemy of our souls. Intercede for us with the Most High that we, too, may courageously fight for the cause of truth and the good of the Kingdom.

Gabriel, Angel of the Incarnation

The angel Gabriel is the great Proclaimer — Proclaimer of the coming Messiah.

There is a description of him in the Book of Daniel. He was, it says,

A man dressed in linen, with a girdle of pure gold
round his waist;
his body like beryl,
his face shone like lightning,

his eyes were like fiery torches, his arms and his legs
had the gleam of burnished orange,
the sound of his voice was like the noise of a crowd.
(Dan. 10:6)

This mighty Prince appeared to Daniel as he was pleading with God, confessing his sins and the sins of his people.

Gabriel had come with the answer to his prayer, but it was more than an answer — it was a prophecy concerning the Anointed One — the One who would deliver his people, not only from Babylon, but from their sins (Dan. 9:30).

This glorious Angel must have fought with great valor during the battle in Heaven — fought as Michael did for the Incarnate Word.

His name, Gabriel, means Strength of God, and he gave strength to those to whom he was sent. The sight of this Angel was so glorious that it made Daniel turn pale, altered his appearance, and left him weakened and trembling. But he gave him the strength to stand firm.

The Angel announced the time of Seventy Weeks. The weeks were weeks of years and had reference to more than the return of the people to Jerusalem.

ON GOD, HIS HOME, AND HIS ANGELS

It was a Messianic Prophecy of the coming of the Anointed Prince — Christ. There is also an allusion to the Crucifixion, for the Angel says, "And after the sixty-two weeks an Anointed One will be cut off" (Dan. 9:26).

We must turn, however, to the Gospel of St. Luke to see Gabriel announcing the coming of the Messiah, but this time to a priest named Zechariah.

Zechariah was also pleading, but his pleading was not for his people. His pleading was for a son. His was a silent prayer — a prayer that had gone on for years — a prayer no longer uttered for it had become so entrenched in his heart — he would merely look at God and sigh.

As priest, it fell to his lot to offer incense in the Lord's Sanctuary.

Suddenly, the Angel of the Lord appeared, standing to the right of the altar.

Zechariah, like Daniel, was afraid, but the Angel assures him there is nothing to fear. "Zechariah, do not be afraid; your prayer has been heard" (Luke 1:13). The Angel goes on to tell the old man that his wife would bear him a son — a son who would be great in the sight of the Lord — a son filled with the Holy Spirit from his mother's womb — a son who would have the spirit and power of Elijah—a son who would prepare the way of the Lord.

The Angel Prophesier proclaimed the Precursor.

Unlike Daniel, whose fear ended in strength and faith, Zechariah's fear produced doubt. He had prayed too long and now that he was old, the sight and prophecy of an Angel brought little hope to him. He looked at the Angel and said, "How can I be sure of this?" (Luke 1:18).

Gabriel is forced to speak the only language Zechariah will understand—a sign—a sign to prove the Angel's mission and power.

"I am Gabriel, who stand in God's Presence, and I have been sent to speak to you and bring you this good news." "Listen," Gabriel continued, "Since you have not believed my words, which will come true at their appointed time, you will be silenced and have no power of speech until this has happened" (Luke 1:20).

Zechariah had doubted the authenticity of the Angel Prophet and the prophecy.

He opened his mouth to speak but no words were uttered. He tried to form words but no sounds came forth. He stood there a long time, half petrified, half ecstatic.

Now he believed, now he would thank God.

The people waiting outside were wondering why it was taking him so long to offer incense, but when he came out and could not speak they realized that he had seen a vision, in the Sanctuary (Luke 1:22).

The sign had a twofold result—it convinced Zechariah of the authenticity of the vision, and it made the people aware that something was about to happen—a feeling of expectation of what was to come.

Six months later, Gabriel came to earth again, and this time he appeared to a virgin living in Nazareth.

He said to her, "Rejoice, so highly favored! The Lord is with you" (Luke 1:28). Scripture says Mary was disturbed at his *words*. Every other time that Gabriel appeared, his appearance struck fear into the beholder, but not this time.

Had this Promised Woman seen him before? Her humility was disturbed by the greeting, but no fear of the Angel himself entered her heart.

Only the truly great are humble—humble enough to know that even though God has been good to them they are still as nothing in comparison to Him. They are those who compare themselves with God and not with other men.

Gabriel was sent by God to announce the Good News: Mary was to conceive and bear a Son—the Son of the Most High (Luke 1:32).

Mary looked perplexed and asked how this would be, and Gabriel continued, "The Holy Spirit will come upon you and the power of the Most High will cover you with its shadow. And so, the Child will be holy and will be called Son of God'" (Luke 1:35, 36).

What was the difference between Zechariah's question, "How can I be sure of this?" and Mary's question, "But how can this come about since I am a virgin?"

We must know, for the question of Zechariah was punished by a loss of speech, and the question of Mary was honored by an explanation.

Zechariah's question stemmed from a soul embittered by disappointment and a lack of faith. He had asked often for a son and received no reply. His knowledge of his own impotency made him doubt it could be done—it was hopeless as far as he was concerned. He needed a dramatic sign to awaken his faith in a God to whom nothing is impossible.

Mary's question was not one of doubt. She did not question that it *could* be done, but as one who was a virgin and intended to remain so, she needed to know *how* it would be done.

Many have questioned Mary's desire to remain a virgin, but if it were not so, why would she ask such a question? She was espoused to Joseph, and if Christ was to be born as other men, the question would indeed have been superfluous.

Mary asked what we must all ask many times during our life span. It is not enough to know *what* God wills, we must also know *how* to fulfill that Will. And this was her question.

Gabriel explained that what was to be born of her was of the Holy Spirit, and Mary united her will to God's, as she said, "I am the handmaid of the Lord; let what you have said be done to me" (Luke 1:38).

And then, Scripture merely states that, "the Angel left her."

This is the last recorded account in Scripture of Gabriel's appearance, but who can doubt that he visited Mary at other times?

Her lack of fear at his appearance makes us believe that it was not the first or the last time she saw him.

The Promised Woman, like all the rest of the human race, would certainly have and need a special Angel to guard her from the snares of the Deceiver. Can we believe that it might be Gabriel—the strength of God—the Angel of the Incarnation?

Raphael, Medicine of God

We learn of the Angel Raphael in a delightful Book in Scripture, the Book of Tobias.

This is an account of a devout Jewish man with strong family ties. It is a beautiful example of parental respect and the action of Divine Providence in daily life.

Though many Bible translations do not include Tobit, the authenticity of its canonical character was established in the years 393, 397, and 697 A.D.

We will look at this account and see how God provides for His children through the mediation of Angels. But before we do, it may be well for us to remind ourselves of what St. Paul said in the Epistle to the Hebrews, "Continue to love each other like brothers, and remember always to welcome strangers, for by doing this, some people have entertained Angels without knowing it" (Heb. 13:1-2). Tobit was a pious Jew who was quite alone in the worship of God, for his tribe and his brothers left the House of Israel and worshipped false gods.

ON GOD, HIS HOME, AND HIS ANGELS

In reading the account of Tobit, we are reminded of Job, who was also an upright man plagued with misfortune. Tobit fed the poor, clothed the naked, buried the dead, and paid tithes of everything he possessed. And then, one day as he sat near the wall in his courtyard, hot sparrow droppings fell into his eyes and blinded him.

Like Job, his wife and friends wondered what good he had derived from his sacrifices and many kind deeds. Had he not been the only loyal member of his family? Everyone but Tobit worshipped alien gods, and now they prospered and he was destitute.

His wife nagged him as she was forced to weave cloth to keep the household.

One day when his wife's insults were especially biting, he sighed and wept for death. As he prayed from the depths of his heart for deliverance from this valley of tears, the great Angel Raphael presented his petitions to God (Tob. 2:14, 3:1-6).

Intercessor

We have here one of the duties of a guardian angel — intercessor.

He is a friend, and real friends pray for their loved ones and their needs.

To pray for others is a spiritual work of mercy, and St. Paul reminds us often of the duty that Christians have of praying for one another.

If this is true of Christians, it is even more true of those spirits whose duty is to care for our welfare.

Raphael said to Tobit, "It was I who offered your supplications before the glory of the Lord and who read them; so, too, when you were burying the dead."

We see here an Angel in action. We are not to think that God has to be informed of our needs by an Angel. We are speaking of the Angel's love and concern for our welfare—the same concern a brother has for a brother—a brother whose love is deep enough to plead his case with his father.

The Angel Raphael was not only conscious of Tobit's plea for help and repeated that plea to God, he also brought before the Most High the good works Tobit had accomplished during his whole life.

Raphael continued, "When you did not hesitate to get up and leave the table to go and bury the dead man, I was sent to test your faith" (Tob. 12:13).

ON GOD, HIS HOME, AND HIS ANGELS

There are many people who accomplish great works of mercy without fanfare or notice. The Sacred Author of Tobit wants us to know that everything we do is known by God, and if He wishes us to do great things for the Kingdom it is necessary to test our ability and humility.

If we prove faithful in small things, He will give us greater things to do.

A Concerned Angel

During Tobit's better days he had deposited ten talents of silver in the safe keeping of Gabael in Rhages.

He decided to send his son, Tobias, to Rhages to withdraw the money, but was fearful for his son's safety on such a journey.

He asked Tobias to go out and find a man he could hire as companion and guide for the journey.

Here we have an account of God's intervention in our daily lives. His Providence cares for every detail of our lives to the point of sending a special Angel to our aid if it is necessary.

Unlike Gabriel and Michael, whose appearances are portrayed as radiant and glorious, Raphael takes on the appearance of a traveler—a man acquainted with Rhages and its direction.

Raphael acts like an ordinary man who has been to Rhages many times, and knows the very man Tobias is to visit. He goes so far as to call himself "a brother Israelite," and agrees to accompany Tobias to Rhages.

The Sacred Author is not trying to overwork our imaginations, but is merely depicting one of the many services a Guardian Angel may exercise in our regard.

While other Angels foretell great events in graphic or symbolic language, Raphael was down to earth. He was interested in everyday problems and every facet that affects the life and happiness of his charge.

It makes us realize the different personalities, and intelligences, and missions of the Angels. We saw Michael as Warrior, Gabriel as a Proclaimer, and now we see Raphael, an Angel interested enough in human affairs to do something about them.

As we read in the Book of Tobit, we find Raphael

- an *Intercessor*, offering Tobit's petitions to God,
- a *Friend*, who remembers Tobit's good works,

- ✎ a *Companion*, ready to protect his charge on a perilous journey,
- ✎ a *Physician*, bringing healing remedies to Sara, Tobias' future wife,
- ✎ a *Deliverer*, binding Satan in hell,
- ✎ a *Healer*, who restored Tobit's sight,
- ✎ and a *Counselor*, advising father and son to thank God for His Goodness to them.

Throughout the Book of Tobit we see Raphael taking care of Tobias in a most marvelous way. Tobias' father had been faithful to God and remained faithful during his trials. God would take care of him and bring good out of the afflictions he endured.

When Raphael finally tells Tobit who he is, he advises him to bless God for all the good things that happened to him. Raphael's concern is that the credit be given to the One to whom it is due — God.

Raphael was merely a messenger, a fellow servant, who did what he did because it was God's Will.

He told them, "I am Raphael, one of the Seven Angels who stand ever ready to enter the Presence of the Glory of the Lord. Do not be afraid: peace be with you. Bless God forever.

As far as I was concerned, when I was with you, my presence was not by any decision of mine, but by the Will of God; it is He whom you must bless throughout your days, He that you must praise. You thought you saw me eating, but that was appearance and no more. Now bless the Lord on earth and give thanks to God. I am about to return to Him above who sent me" (Tob. 11:15-20).

The Sacred Author of Tobit, in an effort to solve the mystery of suffering, gave us an example of the Providence of God and the ministry of His Spirits. It is good to know we are loved and cared for by an Infinite God and powerful Angels.

Comforters

Fallen mankind is often in need of comfort. We are harassed on every side by visible and invisible foes, and our strength gives way under the stress of the battle.

It might be well for us to look in Scripture and find occasions when His ministering Angels raised up the drooping spirits of their earthly brothers.

We have established the existence of Israel's Guardian Angel, whose name was Michael. Looking in the Book of Exodus, we find him at work comforting the Israelites when fear had all but petrified them.

The Israelites had left Egypt only to find themselves pursued by Pharoah and his army. It is written that "the Angel of God, who had been leading Israel's camp, now moved and went around behind them. The column of cloud also, leaving the front, took up its place behind them, so that it came between the camp of the Egyptians and that of Israel" (Exod. 14:19, NAB).

In reading this account, we are so often amazed at God's wonderful care of His People, by protecting them Himself in the form of a cloud, that we skim over the fact that Israel's Guardian Angel also assisted Yahweh in the comforting of this people.

We read in the First Book of Kings that after Elijah had had Jezebel's pagan priests slain, she sent the Prophet a message, saying "May the gods do this to me and more, if by this time tomorrow I have not made your life like the life of one of them" (1 Kings 19:1-2). Poor Elijah was frightened and fled for his life. He walked all day in the wilderness, and finally, exhausted and discouraged, he sat under a furze bush and prayed for death.

He had shown the people the true God, slain the pagan priests, and the only reward he received for his zeal was more trouble and distress. With all his effort, neither the people, himself, nor the cause of God were any better.

Then it was that he fell asleep under the stupor of despair, and an Angel touched him and said, "Get up and eat" (1 Kings 19:5).

Elijah woke up and "at his head was a scone baked on hot stones, and a jar of water" (1 Kings 19:6). His discouragement, however, was so great that he merely got up, ate it, and went back to sleep.

But a second time the Angel touched him, and this time said, "Get up and eat, or the journey will be too long for you. So he got up and ate and drank, and, strengthened by that food, he walked for forty days and forty nights, until he reached Horeb, the mountain of God" (1 Kings 19: 6, 8). It is remarkable in this, and many other accounts, to see the Angels so thoughtful of the human needs of men. They are not only interested in our spiritual welfare but concerned over our physical needs—needs that they themselves do not possess. They realize what we often forget—that man is part animal and part spiritual. And though he is asked by God to keep his mind in

Heaven, his body is very much on earth, and that body needs food, rest, relaxation, and quiet to rebuild itself, that it may continue in its quest for the Kingdom.

The Angels are truly brothers, ready to comfort us on our level, not theirs, patiently waiting until we take courage, and prodding us along when we become disheartened.

We see another incident in the Book of Daniel of their concern in regard to our human needs. Daniel had been thrown into the lions' pit because of his refusal to worship alien gods.

The lions were starved for seven days, and the King fully expected Daniel to be eaten up immediately. Daniel was in the pit six days when an Angel, seeing the Prophet Habakkuk carrying a meal to the reapers, quickly transported him to the lions' den and gave the meal to Daniel.

On the seventh day, the King went to the pit to weep over Daniel, only to find him calmly sitting among the lions. The King was amazed, and rejoiced as Daniel told him that an Angel of the Lord sealed the lions' jaws, and saved the one who loved God so faithfully (Dan. 6:20-23).

This account may sound a little exaggerated, but perhaps we find it unbelievable because our faith in an Omnipotent

God is weak. Does our pride rebel against God sending Angels to intervene in life's tragedies?

Was not the Deacon Philip transported by the Holy Spirit to the carriage of a eunuch?

Yes, God can and does help those who love Him, both by His direct intervention and through His ministering spirits. Our God is a God of Mystery. We have only to praise the Power and Love He manifests towards all His children.

We read in the Gospel of St. Luke that Jesus went to the Garden of Olives with His Apostles. He took Peter, James, and John aside and then went on ahead to pray.

He threw Himself on a rock in great anguish of spirit as He saw what was to come. He prayed an hour and went back to His Apostles for some comfort but found none, for they were asleep.

Three times He asked them to watch and pray with Him, but, like Elijah, their discouragement had dulled their minds and they fell asleep from "sheer grief" (Luke 22:45).

This was the only time in His life He asked for comfort—comfort from human beings—and they failed Him. St. Luke, however, says that He prayed longer and His sweat became like drops of blood: then it was that an Angel appeared to Him to give Him strength.

ON GOD, HIS HOME, AND HIS ANGELS

We are reminded of the Angel that appeared to Elijah and gave him strength for his arduous journey. Did the angel give Jesus a scone to eat, or did he comfort Him with the food of encouraging words? For Jesus Himself told us that man does not live by bread alone but by every word that comes from the mouth of God. Another time He said that His food was to do the Will of Him who sent Him.

Comforting words are indeed food for our souls — food that brings solace, strength, courage, determination, and zeal.

Yes, an Angel of the Lord comforted his Lord by encouraging words — words of the Father's Will, the redemption of mankind, and the holiness of men and women throughout the centuries who would reap the fruit of His suffering by glorifying the Father for all Eternity.

After His Death and Resurrection, we see Angels again, and their role is one of comfort. When the women went to the tomb to anoint the Lord's Body, there was a violent earthquake, and suddenly they saw an Angel of the Lord come down from Heaven, roll away the stone, and sit upon it (Matt. 28:2-6).

St. Matthew says his face was like lightning and his robe white as snow (Matt. 28:3). Suddenly, two men in brilliant clothes stood beside them and said, "Why look among the dead for someone who is alive? He is not here; He is risen" (Luke 24:5).

Were the two Angels that stood beside the women the same two that suddenly appeared after the Ascension? In the Acts we read that as the Lord rose up into the heavens and the Apostles were gazing up into the sky, two men in white stood near them and said, "Why are you men from Galilee standing here looking into the sky?" (Acts 1:9-11).

The Angels must ever question our incredulity and the doubts that take possession of our hearts. We are so slow to believe our great God.

These and many other appearances of Angels in Scripture manifest their deep concern for our needs and spiritual welfare. They have but one desire, and that is, to help us on our journey Home.

Fallen Angels

We say that God created pure spirits like Himself, and we call these spirits "Angels" when they are sent with a message. They are then spirits by nature and Angels by mission.

ON GOD, HIS HOME, AND HIS ANGELS

Can we then address the spirits who rebelled against God, as fallen angels? Yes because they, too, are sent — sent by Lucifer with a message — a message that is false — a message that is a lie.

We must recall what Jesus said about their leader — that he was the father of lies, and "when he lies, he is drawing on his own store" (John 8:44).

These messages are in the form of thoughts — thoughts of despair, sadness, anger, resentment, hate, lust, greed, and jealousy.

It does not mean that every thought of this kind is inspired by the fallen angels. Our own fallen nature can create havoc in our souls an entire lifetime without the help of a fallen angel.

But it does mean that when the angel of darkness sees our temperament and its weaknesses, he uses our frailties to his advantage.

- When he sees sensitiveness, he inspires jealousy.
- When he sees us angry, he inspires hatred.
- When he sees an offense, he inspires resentment.
- When he sees us succeed, he inspires pride.
- When he sees us fail, he inspires despair.
- When he sees us ambitious, he inspires greed.

Whatever weaknesses we possess, we may be sure that he will try to use them to destroy us.

St. Peter reminds us in his First Epistle to "be calm but vigilant, because your enemy, the devil, is prowling round like a roaring lion looking for someone to devour" (1 Pet. 5:8).

Our poor human nature is such that failure and success, sickness and health, persecution and persecutors, anger and patience, are all part of daily life. It is not these weaknesses that cause our falls, but the way in which we use them.

- The consequence of a sin can be either repentance and humility or pride and despair.
- The consequence of being offended can be either forgiveness or revenge.
- The consequence of success can be either gratitude or greed for more.
- The consequence of failure can be either humility mixed with confidence in the future or sadness mixed with despair of any future.
- The consequence of remembering the past can be either gratitude for the good and mercy for the bad or pride in the good and resentment for the bad.

ON GOD, HIS HOME, AND HIS ANGELS

Before Redemption, man was engaged in an uneven battle with the spirit of this world. He could see no good in his weaknesses, and strove with all his strength for success.

The survival of the fittest was an unwritten law that made human life and suffering of little account. We would say then that, with the exception of a small group of people called "Israelites," the angel of darkness was in control and ruled as the Prince of this world—a name Jesus gave him several times.

Though the faithful Angels no doubt tried to aid the people of all nations, they must have had little cooperation. But with Redemption, man himself, possessing the Holy Spirit in his soul, became a veritable bulwark of strength against his invisible foes.

He is no longer alone; the good Angels are no longer fighting a losing battle; Jesus has merited grace, strength, and power for all His children—qualities of soul that would one day make them citizens of Heaven and brothers of the holy Angels.

Armed with Faith, Hope, and Love, and grounded in humility, man, in union with his brothers and fellow servants in the heavenly hosts, can fight the good fight for the Glory of God and the good of the Kingdom.

But we still have an enemy—an enemy who seeks to put us back to the time before Redemption—a time of helplessness and hopelessness.

He ever seeks to destroy our joy by instilling sadness and encouraging distressing thoughts about the past and fears in regard to the future.

The battle we fight on earth is similar to the one fought in Heaven: it is a battle of thoughts, ideas, and desires.

Perhaps this is the reason we are blinded as to the influence of the enemy in our lives. Our thoughts seem to be totally our own, and yet, we are often surprised at the degree of hatred and ill temper we are capable of manifesting.

We cannot excuse ourselves and blame the devil for our actions, but neither can we completely disregard his influence on what is already weak and sinful.

The truth is that the devil cannot force our will to do anything. Man's will is his own, and even God will not interfere with its freedom.

The higher faculties of the soul—the will and understanding—are areas where God alone can penetrate and live. Man opens the door to these inner chambers and lets His Lord dwell therein.

ON GOD, HIS HOME, AND HIS ANGELS

The knob to that door is on the inside, and only its occupant can give entrance to his Lord.

But there are other faculties — memory and imagination — that both good and evil forces can influence, and it is in these areas that man must be ever watchful.

The spirit of darkness seeks to sow seeds of anger, hate, lust, and greed in these two areas. It is here that, unless the enemy is held in control, he breaks down the door of our will and strengthens his influence over us.

We can see this personified in Judas. He was called to be an Apostle; he was given powerful gifts to heal, cure, deliver, and baptize, and yet he permitted his imagination to run wild — wild with dreams of being the right-hand man of the Messiah King who would destroy the enemies of God's People and set up a new kingdom which he, Judas, would help to govern.

Throughout the Scriptures we see him murmuring and complaining — complaining about the sinner anointing the feet of Jesus and seeking for an opportunity to betray his Master.

Jesus, knowing his thoughts, said one day to His Apostles, "Have I not chosen you, you Twelve? Yet, one of you is a devil" (John 6:70). It was a warning, but, like most of us, Judas did not heed the warning.

He kept entertaining thoughts in his mind as to all the things he wished Jesus would accomplish, and then every time the Master spoke of a spiritual Kingdom, he hated Him more.

So we have in Judas a good example of fallen human nature—proud, egotistical, ambitious, and greedy.

Many times Jesus warned him. Many times He gave him special marks of love. "Friend," He said in the Garden, "for what purpose hast thou come?" (Matt. 26:50).

What happened to Judas? What happens to us? Why does Jesus constantly warn us to pray lest we are tempted?

Why did Paul say to the Corinthians, "We live in the flesh, of course, but the muscles that we fight with are not flesh. Our war is not fought with weapons of flesh.... Every thought is our prisoner, captured to be brought into obedience to Christ" (2 Cor. 10:3-5).

Paul had his faults as Judas had his, but the difference is in how each used them and permitted themselves to be used by the Tempter.

Paul strove to control his thoughts and was careful that his thoughts did not control him. He was not ashamed of his weaknesses knowing that God's Power would be more manifest in him. The father of lies then never entered into his house for it was always swept clean with honesty and humility.

Judas, on the other hand, kept on entertaining thoughts of hatred, dislike, and disappointment with Jesus. He excused and rationalized his behavior until the real cause of his misery was no longer himself but Jesus. Jesus, then, must be done away with. He was the cause of this misery. Judas was never honest enough to admit his weaknesses — he mentally reasoned them away. His imagination became overactive, and the memory of the gentle Christ antagonized him.

Every gesture on Christ's part to urge him toward repentance or reform was misinterpreted and turned into more hatred.

A lack of self-knowledge and humility prevented him from seeing any light, and as the darkness became blacker and his will became weaker, he made one final choice that sealed his fate forever. Scripture says that after Jesus gave him a piece of bread that He had dipped, and Judas took it, "at that instant Satan entered him" (John 13:27).

As Satan saw Judas' weaknesses and urged him on, Judas became a man under the control of his emotions and passions. His will and understanding were constantly set aside and he ran his life and thoughts by his greed and ambitions.

Satan prodded him on, and as he shunned the true Light of the World he began to walk in darkness.

Yes, our real foes are invisible; undisciplined mental faculties, and the instigations of the fallen angels, cause hell in this life and the next.

Will we ever be free of our miseries in this life? No. Will the Tempter ever relent in his temptations? No.

But we need never fear, for the Precious Blood of Jesus has been shed that we may partake of His Nature by grace, and with Him in us we can turn ugliness into beauty, lust into purity, greed into detachment, anger into gentleness, and hate into love.

We must remember that the rebel spirits are pure intelligences, pure thoughts — thoughts that insinuate themselves and press upon us, to inflame our fallen nature and weaken our wills.

Our own spirits, however, united to His Spirit, and aided by the angelic spirits, can overcome the enemy and use the very weaknesses that drag us down, to raise us up.

We will always have to conquer those things in us that do not resemble Jesus, but the more control we have of our thoughts, the more peace of mind we shall possess. The mental discipline that comes from the peaceful acceptance of life's trials and tragedies will give us power to overcome the onslaughts of the enemy.

Jesus made a statement that may shed some light on the necessity of mental discipline.

In the Gospel of St. Matthew, He says, "You have learned how it was said, you must not commit adultery. But I say this to you: If a man looks at a woman lustfully, he has already committed adultery with her in his heart" (Matt. 5:28).

This same principle holds true in the case of anger, pride, jealousy, hatred, and many other evils.

Our human nature makes us prone to all these bad qualities, and the Lord knows of what we are made, and so He warns us not to entertain these kinds of sentiments.

If we have been offended and our memory keeps recalling the offense and our imagination continues to exaggerate it, then we are entertaining thoughts of anger. It is at this point that the father of lies, seeing our preoccupations and emotional imbalance, begins to aggravate the condition by recalling other situations that caused us distress. Before we are aware of it, our souls are in such turmoil that it is near impossible to restore any semblance of peace or tranquility.

This is why Jesus asked His Apostles to pray lest they enter into temptation.

Prayer raises our thoughts to God, to the Kingdom, and to Jesus.

Prayer keeps our memory and imagination quiet and under control.

Prayer strengthens our will and enlightens our understanding.

We find many of the holy men and women in Scripture receiving the visitations of the glorious Angels during their time of prayer or in their dreams. It was a time when the higher faculties of the soul were not being harassed by unbridled emotions — a time when the soul could find its God in silence and solitude.

The fallen angels seek to find us off our guard and then they deluge us with thoughts and imaginings that bring our souls down to their level.

Though the holy Angels counteract the inspirations of the enemy by instilling thoughts that lead to kindness and love, the final choice of our direction rests with ourselves.

Countless times in a single day we make small and big decisions — decisions that either strengthen our will or weaken it. Though we fail often, there is one weapon we have that is a terror to the enemy, and that is humility.

An honest acknowledgement of our weaknesses, sincere repentance, and an effort towards greater self-control, all mixed with prayer are a formula for overcoming our faults and dispelling the evil forces that seek to keep our souls in the darkness of their abode.

We will look at the fruit of the enemy and the fruit of the Spirit and will then know which kind of Spirit has the greatest influence over our lives.

FRUIT OF THE SPIRIT

Love, joy, peace, patience kindness, goodness, trustfulness, gentleness, self-control, modesty, chastity, and continency, faith, hope, and true devotion (Gal. 5:22).

FRUIT OF THE ENEMY

Fornication, gross indecency, sexual irresponsibility, idolatry, sorcery, feuds, wrangling, jealousy, bad temper, quarrels, disagreements, factions, envy, drunkenness, and orgies (Gal. 5:19-21).

Such are the fruits we bear, and the seeds of these fruits are sown by good or evil spirits. Our understanding is the ground into which they are thrown, and our wills are the power that push the seed through to bear either good or bad fruit. Though our memory and imagination may at times cause rain and storm, we can still bear good fruit, irrespective of the seed that is sown.

Thousands upon Thousands

In speaking of the Throne of God, Daniel says, "A thousand thousand waited on Him, and ten thousand times ten thousand stood before Him" (Dan. 7:10).

St. John also speaks of great numbers of Angels when he says, "I heard the sound of an immense number of Angels gathered round the Throne.... there were ten thousand times ten thousand of them, and thousands upon thousands shouting, 'The Lamb that was sacrificed is worthy to be given power, riches, wisdom, strength, honour, glory, and blessing'" (Rev. 5:11-12).

Recalling what John says in the Twelfth Chapter of Revelation — that Lucifer took with him one-third of the stars of heaven, the number of the two-thirds that remained faithful staggers the mind.

Jesus Himself said in the Garden of Olives, "Do you think that I cannot appeal to My Father, who would promptly send more than twelve legions of Angels to My defence?" (Matt. 26:53).

ON GOD, HIS HOME, AND HIS ANGELS

Our minds easily tire as we contemplate the sizes and number of stars, planets, galaxies, and quasars. But how much more would they tire if we ever attempted to contemplate the numbers, species, degrees, and missions of the Angelic Hosts!

As star differs from star in the universe, so spirit differs from spirit, and Scripture gives us nine different choirs of Angels. Each one in these choirs is different as each one's degree of intelligence is totally his own, and each one gives glory to God in a way that is uniquely his own. "Lift your eyes and look. Who made these Stars if not He who drills them like an army, calling each one by name?" (Isa. 40:26).

As we search the Scriptures we find these nine choirs of Angels performing different functions. It is only through these functions that we can arrive at any conception of their degree of ascension to the Throne of God.

Seraphim

The choir nearest the Throne of God—meaning those pure spiritual beings most like God—burning of love—seem to be the Seraphim.

We see them in the Sixth Chapter of Isaiah. "I saw the Lord Yahweh seated on a high throne; His train filled the sanctuary; above Him stood seraphs, each one with six wings: two to cover his face, two to cover its feet, and two for flying" (Isa. 6:1-2).

They cried to one another: "Holy, Holy, Holy is Yahweh Sabaoth. His Glory fills the whole earth" (Isa. 6:3).

Isaiah was frightened because the voice of the One who cried out shook the foundations of the threshold and the whole Temple was filled with smoke. In the Presence of God and these exalted creatures, Isaiah became very conscious of his unworthiness. He confesses his uncleanness before all the Heavenly Court, and then one of the Seraphs took a pair of tongs, picked up a live coal from the fire, and touched the lips of the Prophet.

So close was Isaiah to the Fount of Love that his soul was cleansed as in a fire, purified, and made holy.

The Seraphs are always pictured in art as burning flames, ever chanting God's praises, entirely consumed in the glorification of God Who alone is Holy and Who alone is Lord. We must ask them to teach us how to love God with our whole heart, mind, strength, and soul — to give ourselves and become enraptured with God every moment of our lives.

Cherubim

It is difficult to describe spirits, and to describe the missions of those invisible beings is nearly impossible. And yet, to give adequate glory to God, both their existence and work had to be described.

Ezechiel was confronted by this dilemma and so he used a description of something the people of his day had knowledge and understanding of. He used a Babylonian Karibu. It was a half-human, half-animal little god who stood guard at the great temple entrance.

It is difficult for us to imagine any created nature above us, and so our limitations constrain us to describe these glorious spirits in a coarse and faltering language, picturing and symbolizing their natures and work with picturesque but often abstract images.

The Cherubim are especially misunderstood, and yet they are mentioned seventy-four times in Scripture, always hovering over and carrying the Throne of the Most High.

Where the Seraphim seem most like God—flames of love—the Cherubim seem to be occupied with the Glory of God. "I saw," Ezechiel says, "that above the cherubs' heads there was something that looked like a sapphire, and there showed above them the semblance of a throne.... The Glory of Yahweh rose off the Cherubs—the noise of the Cherubs' wings—like the thunder of God Almighty when He speaks" (Ezek. 10:1-2, 5).

The Cherubim are concerned with the proper worship of God and watchful that only those worthy ever enter the Holy of Holies. St. Paul describes the first Holy of Holies and how those who offered sacrifice entered only the outer tent; and once a year, entered the second tent (Heb. 9).

Scripture gives the impression that until Christ the Great High Priest, had come and entered the sanctuary, taking with Him His own Blood for the redemption of mankind, the Cherubim rendered God praise and honor and glory.

It was as if on top of the Ark of the Covenant the Cherubs were spread over—to protect, hold, and render due homage until the Lamb of God came to offer Himself "a perfect sacrifice to God through the Eternal Spirit" (Heb. 9:14).

ON GOD, HIS HOME, AND HIS ANGELS

Thrones, Dominations, Authorities, Sovereignties, and Powers

In the Epistle to the Colossians, St. Paul says that "Christ is the image of the unseen God." For, in Christ, were created "all things in heaven and earth; everything visible and invisible" (Col. 1:16).

It is here that Paul enumerates four of the choirs of Angels. He names the Thrones, Dominations, Sovereignties, and Powers as some of the invisible beings created for Christ (Col. 1:16).

St. Peter exults in the realization that Christ is above everything and sits at God's right hand, making Angels, Dominations, and Powers His subjects (1 Pet. 3:22).

In the eyes of the Sacred Authors, these choirs were beings of great strength and power, and they rejoiced that their Master was Lord over them all.

Paul takes great pleasure in telling his converts that the Power of God manifested itself when He used it to raise Christ from the dead and made Him sit at His right hand "far above every Sovereignty, Authority, Power and Domination" (Eph. 1:21).

Archangels and Angels

St. Paul tells us in the First Epistle to the Thessalonians that "at the trumpet of God, the voice of the Archangel will call out the command, and the Lord Himself will come down from Heaven" (1 Thess. 4:16).

Will this great Archangel be Michael? It seems the name is reserved for him for he is called by Saint Jude, "the Archangel Michael" (Jude 1:9).

The name "Archangel" seems to be reserved, however, for a particular choir.

When Gabriel was being restrained by the Prince of the Kingdom of Persia, he refers to Michael as "*one* of the leading Princes" (Dan. 10:13).

Since both Gabriel and Raphael introduced themselves as "one of the Seven who stand in God's Presence" (Tob. 12:15, Luke 1:19), we can safely surmise that these two Spirits are also Archangels — great Princes in the Heavenly Hierarchy — entrusted by God with exalted missions.

The times that the choir of Angels is mentioned in Scripture are too numerous to describe. It may suffice to look at St.

ON GOD, HIS HOME, AND HIS ANGELS

Luke's Gospel and read how an Angel of the Lord appeared to Shepherds and announced the Birth of Christ:

> And suddenly with the Angel there was a great throng of the Heavenly Hosts praising God. (Luke 2:13)

So we have in Scripture nine choirs of Angelic Spirits: Seraphim, Cherubim, Thrones, Dominations, Powers, Authorities (sometimes called Virtues), Sovereignties (sometimes called Principalities), Archangels, and Angels.

There is a beautiful passage in St. Luke's Gospel that many Christians during the first few centuries of the Church felt was indicative of the number of the Angelic Hosts.

Jesus told the crowds one day that if a man had a hundred sheep and he lost one, he would leave the ninety-nine and go seek the lost sheep.

And then he would call in his friends that they might all rejoice with him because he found the sheep that was lost. Now we can and usually do apply this to the just and unjust, the just being the ninety-nine and the sinner, the lost sheep.

This may well be the lesson, except that one sentence adds a new dimension. The Master said, "I tell you, there will be more rejoicing in Heaven over one repentant sinner than over ninety-nine virtuous men who have no need of repentance" (Luke 15:4, 7).

Yes, it is true, all Heaven rejoices when a sinner repents, but Jesus said there was more joy than over those who did not need repentance.

All the children of Adam need repentance no matter how virtuous they are. St. John says, "If we say we have no sin in us, we are deceiving ourselves and refusing to admit the truth.... To say that we have never sinned is to call God a liar and to show that His Word is not in us" (1 John 2:8-10).

So then, we all need repentance—all except those pure Spirits who form the Heavenly Hosts. They had one test, they chose God, and they never sinned, so they had no need of repentance. It is no wonder that so many early Christians felt that the ninety-nine referred to by Our Lord as having no need of repentance, were the multitude of Angelic Hosts.

The lost sheep represented to them mankind, who left the way of God and chose the way of the world.

The Good Shepherd left his ninety-nine in Heaven to seek His lost sheep—wayward mankind. When He found it and redeemed it, He took it upon His shoulders and opened the door of the Great Sheepfold where the ninety-nine rejoiced with exceeding great joy.

> After this, I seemed to hear the great sound of a huge crowd in Heaven singing "Alleluia! Victory and Glory and Power to our God."
>
> Then a voice came from the Throne. It said, "Praise our God, you servants of His, and all who, great or small, revere Him.... Let us be glad and joyful and give praise to God, because this is the time for the marriage of the Lamb. His bride is ready, and she has been able to dress herself in dazzling white linen, because her linen is made of the good deeds of the saints."
>
> The Angel said, "Write this: Happy are those who are invited to the wedding feast of the Lamb." ... Then I knelt at His feet to worship Him, but He said to me, "Don't do that: I am a servant just like you and all your brothers who are witnesses to Jesus. It is God that you must worship." Amen. (Rev. 19:1, 5, 8-10)

PRAYER

St. Michael and all you holy Angels, protect us from the snares of the evil spirits. Instill into our minds thoughts of repentance and love, and obtain for us from the Throne of the Most High the Gifts of the Spirit and a bright reflection of Jesus in our souls.

SCRIPTURE

Then, leaving the crowds, He went to the house; and His disciples came to Him and said, "Explain the parable about the darnel in the field to us." He said in reply, "The sower of the good seed is the Son of Man. The field is the world; the good seed is the subjects of the Kingdom; the darnel, the subjects of the evil one; the enemy who sowed them, the devil; the harvest is the end of the world; the reapers are the Angels. When then, just as the darnel is gathered up and burnt in the fire, so it will be at the end of time. The Son of Man will send His Angels and they will gather out of His Kingdom all things that provoke offences and all who do evil, and throw them into the blazing furnace, where there will be weeping and grinding of teeth. Then the virtuous will shine like the sun in the Kingdom of their Father. Listen, anyone who has ears!" (Matt. 13:36-43)

THE HEAVENS

BEFORE TIME BEGAN

An Explanation

This Mini-Book is unlike the other works the Lord has given me to write. The others were born of light, light that was given to me as each book unfolded.

This work is different, for it is the fruit of a spiritual experience. It began one morning after Holy Communion and continued throughout various stages as this book was being written. Each paragraph was lived, so there was much time between writings, as if the experience of each part had to be lived and savored before going on.

I am not sure what benefit or light the reader of these pages will receive. I only pray that some of the same experience will penetrate the souls of all who read it. It is my hope that it will make many understand God's personal choice of them and the burning love He has for each soul He created.

ON GOD, HIS HOME, AND HIS ANGELS

It was written exactly as it was lived and so it may not always be in any particular order of thought. Since I did not understand the experience fully, I was only able to express my feelings rather than the purpose of the reality of being somewhere before time began.

Before Time Began

Lord God, what is this strange experience? My soul seems to stand alone on a huge sphere—a sphere as big as the earth. I stand tall and unafraid and yet I am aware of looking out into nothingness. It is almost as if time reversed itself and I stand in the void before creation. I wait in silence. Although my faculties operate in the midst of daily occupations, joys and distress, my soul is somehow separated from these realities and at the same time immersed within them. All goes on as usual but with a constant awareness of being alone, looking out into a void. There are times my soul cries out "Yahweh" but no answer is heard. While silence is the only response, there is an awareness of Presence. Although this Presence is the God my heart seeks, the distance is vast. Is my sense of

Presence only His Gaze? Is this pure faith, with nothing on which to hang?

I feel as though I were somehow present in the nothingness — in the nonexistence as the ALL looked out into the void before anything was made. What a contrast — the ALL and nothingness. Did nothingness in all its bleak nakedness cry out to God who is Existence Itself and say — without saying — "Let me become — Give me existence"? The void was silent and helpless — waiting. My soul watches God and the void face each other. The feeling of helplessness is overwhelming as I wait in total dependence upon the Word to speak so that nothingness can be. Is this when my soul sings out "Yahweh" in a long cry for life and then waits for the Divine Will to make its decision known? Is this a glimpse of the instant before moments began?

Is this not an exercise in Faith? Sometimes faith places me before nothing that visibly assures me of God's love or concern. But as the void once faced God and waited for existence, my soul waits for that depth of Faith that ever keeps its eyes on the ALL — the Lord, God Almighty. Oh God, let the arms of your omnipotence enfold my nothingness and permit me to see you in Faith.

ON GOD, HIS HOME, AND HIS ANGELS

As I stand alone I find myself facing the void, waiting upon His Voice to speak — waiting for the beginning — feeling alone yet aware of Someone — looking for signs of life, of existence, existence of what seems to be a mere thought of me. It is as if God extracted from His Infinite mind the thought of me that was His before He created anything. He placed that thought — me — on this sphere to wait for existence, in order that I might taste the feeling of my total dependence upon Him for my very breath. Does He want me to feel what it would mean never to have been born — to be humbled at the realization that there was a chance I would never have been?

This experience is a mystery to me — a terrifying waiting period as I face the void. The thought that is me, stands so still, looking around, wondering from whence shall come the Voice that placed me there. Will He make the decision that I will "be" or shall I be merely a thought of what might have been?

The silence is a quiet silence. It is not like the deafening silence that comes suddenly from an absence of noise. The void too is different from the darkness that descends from an absence of light. There is only a sense of Presence for the nothing that is before me has no sound, no being, no existence, no darkness.

I hear the "thought" that is me, cry out again in a long plaintive chant "Yahweh, give me being — give me life — let me live!" Silence is the only response to my cry. I wait, facing the void, knowing that the answer to that plea is hidden — as I was once hidden — in the Infinite Mind of the only Existent One.

This is a truly strange experience. I am here writing this page and yet my soul at times finds itself on that sphere or place where I wait for the Divine decree to decide whether or not I shall be. I have an awareness of being and not being at the same time. Has God somehow placed my soul before time began so I may experience my total dependence upon Him? There are times the Enemy tries to make me believe that this experience is really a vision of my place for all eternity. It then becomes a kind of solitary confinement as if I were to be there forever — separated from God, my loved ones and the entire throng of saints in heaven. Then it is that my soul cries out — "Oh God, if this place is Your decree for me forever, if it would please You to see me here for all eternity, then Your Will be done. Even if you do not hear my voice or are touched by my anguish, still shall I cry out in this shoutless void—'My God, Yahweh, I love You!" I would wish that the sound of that cry of love would somehow pierce the void and reverberate through timeless space and one day reach Your throne. I would be satisfied if somehow You did not know from whence it came. Would it, if that were possible, thrill Your Heart by its sound?

The terrifying thought of never seeing Your Face does not last long, my God, and I realize the Enemy wishes to spoil some work You have begun in my soul. I trust Your judgments, Your Wisdom and Your Love. I am again at peace, gazing into Nothingness—waiting for Someone very distant to return my gaze. I am not aware of Faith, though I'm sure it must be present. Hope is elusive as if it were peeking around some hidden corner of the void, waiting to be discovered. Love—where is love here. There seems to be love in the Presence around me, but as yet it is very general—it does not direct itself to me—there is no point of contact—no thrill of recognition—no natural outpouring as the love within one flows out and touches the love of another to become one love. I wait for Being—for acceptance—for love.

Where is Love and does Love know me? Is there the chance that He will not call me to Be? Am I not guaranteed creation by the fact I am in His Mind? No, it is not true. There is no guarantee. The thought of me that is in His mind must be called forth—He must look at me—discern—make a decision and then choose me to Be. The agony of waiting is beyond expression. When He sees what weaknesses I will possess—what rebellious moments I will indulge in—will the knowledge of His power in weakness override the failures He sees in me? When He sees my feeble efforts to try and try again will that sway His decision in my favor?

I remain looking out into the void but it is somehow different. There is a sudden warmth—a feeling of Someone looking at me. I look around and out into the void and though there is no form that says "Presence," there is a kind of general Presence that is turning toward me. It all happens very slowly and very gently. It is a breathtaking moment. Fear wants to creep in.

Though the experience is new, I already fear the Presence will look, see and then pass me by. It seems the time of decision to choose has come. Has the One to whom I cry out heard my voice? Is He turning my way?

ON GOD, HIS HOME, AND HIS ANGELS

I begin to feel an awareness, an awareness of love. It is attentive, caring, gentle and secure. Though the void still looms ahead, it somehow does not seem important. However, for the first time I am aware of suddenly being in the midst of other "thoughts" that might be. There are millions upon millions of them. The awareness of Love is still here, but it is as though each one of the millions has the same look of attentive love as I have. I am alone, yet not alone. It is possible that they too wish and cry out for being? Will He hear each cry? Will each voice of such a throng reach His ears? Will it be like the mighty roar of an ocean or will each one be heard individually? Will He ever hear my cry in the midst of so many? The number of "thoughts" of possible human beings grows from millions to billions. I am surrounded by so many, who like myself, cry out for Being.

Every moment of this experience brings with it the realization that my chances for life are getting slimmer by the minute. I am immersed in an ocean of possible human beings and yet I still stand alone on this sphere. He sees me and knows me. I feel no rebellion or anxiety, only a burning desire to Be, to be able to return the care, love and attention I am beginning to feel. I am the recipient of something I cannot return.

I am aware of an unruffled anxiety as I stand in the midst of this shoutless void, seeking an invisible reality. I no longer cry out "Yahweh" for it seems so fruitless. I only wait and wait and wait.

There is a quiet submission in my soul, a kind of dependence that is deeply aware of facing a power beyond my comprehension. The power is without limit and yet gentle. It is as if there were a certain caution in that power, for fear the strength of it might blow me away.

I see a Light. It is separate from the void. It does not take the void away by its presence. It moves gently over all the "thoughts" that might one day be. Is it searching or choosing? It passes over each one as if it saw everything that "thought" might become. How awesome is the sight! As the Light passes from one to another, that thought totally disappears. Does the Light take that thought back into itself or is it totally gone? I see in its place only more of the void—nothingness in the place of what might have been. The Light moves on to another and another. Will it pass me by as it has already done to so many? Those who are passed by shall never be. What was their potential? What might they have done, spoken, written, sung? What multitudes will never be because those who are passed by will never be in a position to give life? I am frightened at the awesome reality of the gift that life is, in the face of this experience.

As the Light moves from one to another, I do not see even one remain. They are disappearing by the millions. I begin to perceive a new warmth. The Light is coming closer. I am no longer frightened. I wait in peace as every "thought" is replaced by more and more of the void. It happens quickly and yet never seems to end. There are so many, but the Light touches each one as it sweeps over them all.

I am conscious of possessing three faculties. They are empty, however, as if brand new. There are no feelings that a body possesses—only all thought—as if my soul were being formed by light as it nears the "thought" of me. Yes, something is happening as the Light comes nearer to me. There are three distinct faculties forming. There is not three of me, but the thought of me is now capable of three distinct operations. I know I have the ability to remember, though there is nothing to recall. I can reason, but the Light is beyond my comprehension. I can choose, but there are no choices to make.

I feel akin to the Light. It is as if we were somehow alike. Has the Presence only made me see what the thought of me really is? No, the Light is coming closer. I see others disappear before me, around me, above me, beneath me. I am alone. The Light envelops me and covers me with its Shadow. For the first time I hear a Voice say, "You shall be." I am astounded, surprised, grateful. I am not able to respond. Infinite Love has made a decision—I shall be! It is hard to believe. Every other thought that might have been, just totally disappeared and I have been chosen to be. Why me? Why me? I am grateful and humbled by the choice.

I see the Light that decided my existence begin to move out and cover the void and the same Voice that said, "You shall be," says, "Let there be light" and a different kind of light appears, far inferior to the Light that is power.

Yes, one day, after millions of years, the thought of me in the mind of God will take form. He will fit me with a body. The memory, intellect and will that was given to me as a gift will be mine to use freely as I will. I will have the opportunity to make choices in His favor as He made one in mine. I will live and love and be loved. I will see beauty, hear sounds, discern and form opinions, cry and laugh, experience the thrill of learning and the joy of sharing. I shall live in a specific time in history and make a print in its sand of time. I shall be a part of a whole, a member of the human race.

I continue to stand on the sphere with assurance instead of doubt. It is now a place of wonder—a place where the soul and God live alone, a place of rest and contentment; a place where everything is seen for what it is outside of God, a place to face the truth and speak to God as a friend speaks to a friend, a place to wait upon His Will. I thank you, Oh God, for this experience of faith, of Your love and the gift of life.

My parents said, "Amen—so be it."

The End

The experience you have just read is over. Looking back I am only now aware that it was given to me to make a point of knowledge, a reality. It brought home God's personal love and choice of me. When He created my soul in my mother's womb, the thought of me, in His mind before time began, became a reality.

I shall cherish this experience and pray that all those who read it will somehow understand that special choice. I am sure some aspects of this book are not clear, but that is due to an inability to clearly portray the mysterious.

We praise Him for all those He has created and chosen to be. We admire His wisdom and stand awestruck at the sight of His Love.

Inside the Kingdom

Something to Think About

The first letter Paul wrote to his converts was one addressed to the Thessalonians. It was sixteen or seventeen years after his conversion, as he traveled with Silas and Timothy, that it seemed necessary to explain the Kingdom and the Second Coming of Jesus to these new and faithful converts.

The Second Coming—the Kingdom—Heaven—all these are words that are abstract and distant to most Christians. We have been told about it so often and waited so long that what should be an interior, anticipated joy has become a doubtful, imaginary tale, designed to scare us into virtue.

There are few things we anticipate with longing that ever come up to our expectations, but only because the things we desire are earthly, and by their very nature, temporary. Anything passing is already on its way out the moment we possess it.

ON GOD, HIS HOME, AND HIS ANGELS

We almost feel it leaving our grasp as we lay hands on it, and this feeling of elusiveness mars our perfect joy. So it is with everything the world has to offer, and yet—we cling to this kind of happiness, frustrated by its transitory nature, and yet fascinated by its passing joys.

We forget this kind of happiness is a mere oasis in the desert of life—it is not our final resting place—only a short stay that is designed to refresh our souls with a taste of what is to come.

All earthly joys are finite glimpses of eternal bliss. But because we tend to hold on to what we see with our physical eyes, we tend to forget what can be seen only with the eyes of Faith. And so it is that Heaven is always remote from our thoughts and removed from our daily experiences.

To most of us, the effort necessary to keep Heaven in our minds and hearts is just too much. We would rather take the line of least resistance and concentrate on visible things. We can easily forget their temporary nature and pretend they are permanent by throwing ourselves into them. But somehow there is always a small corner of our souls in a vacuum—a vacuum that only God and Heaven can fill. For that vacuum we praise His holy Name.

The first Christians Paul wrote to had lived in a vacuum for years. They tried everything from idolatry to debauchery to fill it, but never did. When they heard Paul speak of the Messiah, His Death and Resurrection, a seed of Faith was sown into their hearts, which bore the fruit of peace and fulfillment.

They began to live by the Faith given to them and they longed to see this Jesus—see Him triumph over His enemies and come again.

The Second Coming created another vacuum in their souls. However, this vacuum was not a painful air pocket but a large capacity for God—a capacity that became greater as it was filled, and filled as it became greater.

They possessed a longing to see Jesus, to be united to Him, and to enter the Kingdom. Everything they did, from early morning to late at night, was done in a spirit of detachment and expectation. This gave them a buoyant Hope which nothing could dampen. Some of them literally lived on this Hope so much so that they refused to work, and Paul had to correct them with severity (2 Thess. 3:6-15).

Almost two thousand years have passed since these Christians looked forward to the Second Coming. Each one of them, and millions after, have all seen the Lord Jesus face to face at that beautiful time we call Death.

Although the Second Coming did not arrive in their lifetime, they will experience it when it comes. Paul tells us that they will also witness the Second Coming along with those who are alive at that time.

He told the Thessalonians, "We want you to be quite certain, brothers, about those who have died, to make sure you do not grieve about them, like the other people who have no hope" (1 Thess. 4:13).

These zealous Christians were so excited over Jesus coming again, they were afraid those who had died would miss the glory of it all. But Paul assured them, "We believe that Jesus died and rose again, and that it will be the same for those who have died in Jesus: God will bring them with Him" (1 Thess. 4:14).

The souls of those who have died in the Lord and been in His Presence in His Kingdom, will accompany the Lord when He returns, and they will be the first to be united to their glorified bodies. "At the trumpet of God, the Archangel will call out the command, and the Lord Himself will come down from Heaven; those who have died in Christ will be the first to rise, and then those of us who are still alive will be taken up in the clouds together with them, to meet the Lord in the air" (1 Thess. 4:16-17).

The souls of the just, having been with their Lord and enjoyed His Kingdom, will take possession of their bodies — new and glorified — and there will be a new Heaven — a Heaven inhabited by human beings. From the time of their death to the Second Coming only their souls were with God, but now they will be like Jesus — Resurrected — body and soul.

People have argued for centuries about Heaven. Some say it is a place, and others say it is a state, but Scripture indicates it is both. It tells us in many places the Kingdom of Heaven is "within" us and "among" us. And Jesus tells us, "No one has gone up to Heaven except the One who came down from Heaven, the Son of Man who is in Heaven" (John 3:13).

Here we have a clear indication that Heaven is both a place and a state of soul. Jesus came down *from* Heaven, and because of His union with the Father, He was *in* Heaven.

And so it is with us. When we keep His Word, He makes His home in us, and that is a Heaven on earth — the Kingdom within us (John 14:23).

When we die and our souls leave our bodies to await the Second Coming, Jesus promised us a place to live, "I am going now to prepare a place for you, and after I have gone and prepared you a place, I shall return to take you with Me: so that where I am, you may be too" (John 14:2-3).

At death, we see Jesus face to Face. He comes for us, because all during our life, through joys and sorrows, He prepares a place of glory for us in His Kingdom. He used everything to change us to His Image, and we shall take our places in the Kingdom according to the clarity of His Features in our souls. There are many rooms in His Father's House, and glory will differ from glory as star differs from star.

Jesus used many parables to show us what the Kingdom of Heaven is like, but most of them seem like only the frame of a building—a building not finished or furnished.

The reason for this is that the Lord is speaking of different aspects or parts of the same Kingdom of Heaven. Wherever God is, there is Heaven, and since God is everywhere, then Heaven is everywhere.

But we must remember that Jesus speaks of the Kingdom of Heaven *within* us, *around* us, and *above* us.

There are not three Heavens—only one Heaven. We live in the first two phases during our earthly pilgrimage, and the third—in the Eternal Kingdom.

Our concept of Heaven, with all its glory, and our realization of the misery within and around us, makes the concept of Heaven on earth unreal and exaggerated.

No human mind would ever think there could be such a thing as Heaven on earth. But since Jesus has revealed it, we must see what He means.

In the fourteenth and fifteenth Chapters of St. John's Gospel, Jesus tells us several times that God makes His home in us when we keep His Word. "Anybody who receives My Commandments and keeps them will be one who loves Me; and anybody who loves Me will be loved by My Father, and I shall love him and show Myself to him" (John 14:21).

"God is love," St. John says, "and anyone who lives in love lives in God, and God lives in him" (1 John 4:16). We must possess in our own souls the quality that makes Heaven both a state and a place—Love—God's Love—the Kingdom within us.

The very Nature of God is Love, and our interior spiritual faculties must be changed into Love. We must possess a loving Memory, a loving Intellect, and a loving Will. Our whole being must be like God—Love.

The more our interior is changed by the graces He has given us at Baptism, the more like God we will become. To understand this, we will look at St. Paul and see his concept of the Kingdom "within us" that helps make the Heaven "around us."

Paul tells us no matter how intelligent, gifted, generous, mortified, or full of faith we may be, it is all nothing without Love.

We look at this passage and immediately think of Love as that "feeling" or "emotion" that brings joy to the heart and light to the eyes. And we can understand how all the above things would be lifeless without love. But the love we are thinking of is more than the gratification or satisfaction that comes from being generous, or gifted, or mortified.

Paul's definition of Love is a love that changes us—changes our way of thinking and acting. It is a love that is patient, kind, compassionate, and understanding. It is a love that we may not always experience, but we will always know is present—in our hearts—in our minds—in our souls.

The first thing we think of about Heaven is the Love that reigns there. We will love everyone, and everyone will love us—love us with a completely unselfish love. We will love in the same way God loves.

We shall all be changed from self-centered individuals to God-centered sons. We shall see as we have been seen, and know as we have been known.

Our Will becomes completely and totally united to God —never vacillating or wandering away from the path of God.

Our Memory will be at peace, no longer tormenting us with guilt complexes, resentments, or the recollection of old injuries. It will rejoice over its past weaknesses as it praises the Mercy of God who was so bountiful in its regard.

Our Understanding will comprehend the deepest mysteries with ease, ever delighting in the limitless realms that it can roam, as it constantly learns new things about God and His glorious works.

We shall be free—really free—free from unbridled passions that cause turmoil in our soul—free of those uncontrolled emotions that drive us from exaltation to desperation—free of the possessiveness of friends and the hatred of enemies—free of weaknesses, physical and spiritual, that make us feel inferior and inadequate.

We shall stand tall and unafraid of anyone or anything. Death, and all the separations it imposes, will be gone forever. Fear will be unknown and unfelt in that place. Only perfect peace and loving serenity will be our portion—and that forever.

We shall see God in everyone and everywhere, and the most exalted creatures, the Angelic Hosts, will be our most intimate friends.

Instead of the light of Faith, we shall see God face to Face; instead of Hope for the journey, we shall possess the security of having arrived and being safe forever; instead of an unstable love, we shall be set forever in a deep love for God—a Love that never vacillates or changes.

There will be no problems to solve or face. We shall see everything in its entirety, as it is in God, and then we shall know all the "whys" and "wherefores" of life.

We will be able to see why there was poverty, pain, and suffering in the world; and as we see the undreamed-of good that God brought out of all this evil, we shall praise Him and glorify Him with hearts full of thanksgiving. What was once a sorrow, shall be a source of great joy.

The crippled and maimed will see how God used their deformities and incapacities for their greater good. They will see how God was glorified, and their happiness enhanced by what they thought was a tragedy and an injustice.

This is how it will be in the Heaven above, and St. Paul told us to "look for the things that are in Heaven.... Let your thoughts be on heavenly things, not on the things that are on earth" (Col. 3:1-2). But what do the things to come have to do with everyday human living?

Was Paul giving us some kind of spiritual anesthetic to numb the pains of life? No, he was giving us a goal to look forward to. He was telling us not to be bogged down in the mud of this world — to keep our minds and hearts always lifted up to our real home.

Paul used the thought of Heaven as a tool to keep his hope and courage strong when everything seemed to fall apart. He tried very hard to live in the Christ within his own soul — the "first Heaven." He spoke to the Christians of growing brighter and brighter until they were turned into Jesus, and this was the "second Heaven" — the Heaven among us. But one day — he did not know how — he was brought up into the "third Heaven."

He "heard things which must not and cannot be put into human language" (2 Cor. 12:4). He was brought up to that Heaven where Jesus sits at the right hand of the Father. But immediately after relating this vision, he began to speak of his weaknesses and his sufferings. He kept his thoughts on heavenly things—he realized that his everyday life was somehow bound up in the Kingdom.

He asked those Corinthians to test themselves and see if they were in the faith. He told them that if they did not believe that Jesus Christ was really *in* them, they failed the test.

As great as the revelation of Heaven was, Paul did not lose contact with reality. Christians were "God's new creation," but they had to "prove" they were God's servants and members of the Kingdom by their purity, knowledge, patience, kindness, and a spirit of holiness (2 Cor. 5:16-17).

The Kingdom among us depends upon the Heaven within each member of the Christian community. It must begin "within" before it can reach out to others. There can be no compromise between good and evil—virtue and vice.

We must make choices every day—choices that direct us toward good or evil. In order to motivate our Will toward the right choices, we must have incentive and knowledge of what is to come.

Our human nature longs for love and to be with the one we love. So it is both natural and supernatural to desire God and Heaven—to desire Love and the possession of that Love—to desire Union and the place where that union is most perfect.

Jesus has asked us to keep the Father's Word that we may live in the Father's House, for this is the purpose of our creation and the end of our pilgrimage.

Jesus never forgot His Father or His Home, so we must follow in His footsteps and see the place to which He leads us.

We will search the Scriptures to find this place, to open its doors, to look inside, to roam its vaults, to see its inhabitants, to learn its secrets, and to feel its joys.

Joys of Heaven

It is difficult for us to envision the joys of Heaven, because all the joys we experience in this life are short-lived. They are tempered by the realization that sorrow usually follows.

But in Heaven this will not be so. Our joy will be complete and eternal. It will never be lessened by any sorrow for sorrow will be no more. "God will wipe away all tears from our eyes; there will be no more death, and no more mourning or sadness" (Rev. 21:4).

When those tears have been wiped away by the Hand of God, we shall gaze into His Face and see what eyes have never seen or imagined. The beauty and joy of that moment is so exquisite that only the immortal soul, separated from the body in death, could gaze upon it and live.

It is a light so bright, and a beauty so ravishing, that the created soul would be annihilated by the sight, had not God given it grace — a divine participation in His own nature — a gift by which it can "carry the weight of eternal glory" (2 Cor. 4:17).

The joy of all joys shall come when God writes His Name on our foreheads, and gives each one of us a name — a name known and understood only by God and our soul (Rev. 22:4; Isa. 62:2).

We shall be as one who has fought the good fight and arrived home to be refreshed and strengthened — not for more combat, but for the reward of victory — victory over sin, weakness, and evil.

In Heaven our joy will be enhanced by the presence of loved ones, old acquaintances, and people we have read about or heard about. We will be happy to see them and they will rejoice over our presence in their midst.

Everyone in Heaven radiates God in a different way and degree. Each one will have that degree of love and union they had at the moment of death. When we die, we cease to merit; we cease to use our talents; it is the time of reward or punishment. Whatever talents we have been given, used, and increased, will be ours for all eternity. We will be rewarded in proportion to the way our free will chose God above ourselves and the world.

This means that our *capacity* for love and joy will be set forever, and so each one of us will radiate Jesus in a different way. We shall receive a "denarius" (Heaven) for our wages, but each one of us will enjoy the glory of Heaven according to his capacity for Love.

It is so in this world. We all live on the same planet Earth, but each one has a different personality, intelligence, virtue, and talents. We have all received the denarius of life, but each one uses that opportunity in a different way.

It is not important what we possess in this world; it is how we use these possessions that counts. Jesus warned us not to judge Heaven by worldly standards, for the "first" here may be the "last" there.

And so, the joy of those who have suffered much will be greater than those who have suffered little. The joy of those who have loved much will be greater than those who have loved less.

ON GOD, HIS HOME, AND HIS ANGELS

Because our joy in Heaven has God for its Source, it will be everlasting in duration and insatiable in capacity. It will always be fresh because there will always be something new to be joyful about.

There will never be anything to mar or lessen our joy because, unlike the joy on earth that springs forth from people and things which are in a constant state of change, this Joy is like God—Changeless, because it springs from an infinite source of beauty and love.

Jesus told His Apostles that "A woman in childbirth suffers because her time has come; but when she has given birth to the child she forgets the suffering in her joy that a man has been born into the world" (John 16:21). And so it shall be in Heaven—no matter how much we have suffered on earth, it will all be turned into joy—a joy so great we will forget the suffering entirely.

We shall have joy in Heaven every time a loved one on earth repents. Jesus told us of this unexpected joy when He gave us the parable of the lost sheep and drachma. When both were found, He said, all of Heaven and all the Angels rejoiced (Luke 15:4-10).

We are not accustomed to being loved that much, but it is this very deep and sincere love that constitutes the unalterable joy of Heaven.

To know that we are loved, totally and without limit, by such a great God and all His sons, will fill our souls with a joy that we cannot conceive on earth.

But what about joy in the Kingdom on earth? Is real joy something we shall experience for the first time in the third Heaven? No, what we see there in vision must be seen here in Faith, and what we experience there as an eternal possession, must be felt here in anticipation—in Hope. Our joy must begin here if it is to be perfected in Heaven.

When the Angel announced the birth of Christ to the Shepherds and the world, he said, "I bring you news of great joy—a joy to be shared by the whole people" (Luke 2:10).

Jesus, then, is our greatest joy on earth—Joy is the sign of the Christian—a sign that speaks loudly to a sad world—a sign of God dwelling in our soul—a sign of union with His Will in our lives—a sign of contradiction in the midst of pain—a sign that a Christian has something and Someone that the world cannot give.

ON GOD, HIS HOME, AND HIS ANGELS

A sad Christian is no Christian, for he must live in God —live in Heaven—and he cannot be sad in that place. He must manifest those eternal qualities of soul here and now, imperfect though they be, to show the world that God is Love and God dwells in us.

Jesus promised us joy on earth when He told us to keep His Father's Commandments out of love. "I have told you this," He said, "so that My own joy may be in you, and your joy be complete" (John 15:11).

He speaks of our joy being "complete" right here on earth amidst untold misery. Yes, when we see God's Will in every incident in our lives, when we seek His love in every person, when we desire to be like Him in all our actions, when we see His Shadow behind every cross, and make every effort to live with Him in the Heaven of our souls—then our joy is complete.

The greatest source of our joy on earth must be in the realization that Christ is Risen! Our God has conquered death —we have a Home to go to when life is over—we can be born again to a new life here and hereafter. "I shall see you again, and your hearts will be full of joy, and *that* joy no one shall take from you" (John 16:22).

Our joy in Heaven will be mixed with happiness, but on earth, happiness eludes us because it is something outside of us. We often think of these two qualities of soul as being alike, but they are different, and though we cannot always be happy, we can always be joyful.

Happiness is a state of soul caused by some exterior happening or person, but since these things are passing, our happiness, too, is passing. There is always something or someone to mar our happiness — it is never complete.

We may be loved by a thousand people, but the hatred of one will make our happiness incomplete. This is not so with joy, for joy springs from within the depths of the soul where God lives. Its source of life is not exterior, but interior, and it finds occasions to manifest itself in every life-situation, pleasant or painful.

Yes, we can be joyful in painful circumstances. Jesus told us to be so when He said, "Blessed are you when people hate you, abuse you, denounce your name as criminal, on account of the Son of Man. Rejoice when that day comes, and *dance for joy*, for then your reward will be great in Heaven" (Luke 6:22-23).

The hope of Heaven is to strengthen us in times of trial, and that Hope must be so authentic that its effect is joy of heart. The pain in itself is not the cause of our joy, but the opportunity to imitate Jesus raises us above the trial at hand. We see God in it — we see His Providence — His Love — His Mercy — and His Power. This enables us to see suffering for what it is — a pruning and healing process to change us into Jesus — Suffering "makes sense" and no longer depresses us, but affords us an occasion to manifest the Power of God in our lives — our joy filled lives.

This is the kind of joy that no one can take away, for it is deep within the soul. This is the kind of joy that prepares our soul for the happiness of Heaven — a constant, quiet joy, welling up from hearts totally given to God by union with His Will. It is the fruit of a great Faith, a Faith that rejoices in whatever its Lord wills.

St. Paul told the Philippians that he would help them make progress in their Faith and increase their joy in it (Phil. 1:25). He told the Colossians that they would have strength, "based on His own glorious Power, never to give in, but to bear anything joyfully" (Col. 1:11).

Faith in Jesus is the cause of our joy, and Faith tells us that God's Hand is guiding our lives, and He permits evil and pain only for our good. St. Peter told the first Christians, "You did not see Him, yet you love Him; and still without seeing Him, you are already filled with a joy so glorious that it cannot be described, because you believe" (1 Pet. 1:8).

The fact that the joy of a Christian is not dependent upon all things going well, but increases in adversity, has proven a stumbling block to some, and a fascinating phenomenon to others.

It is a witness that attracts unbelievers, who are realistic enough to know you cannot obliterate suffering. They wonder how a Christian maintains joy in his trials. It is his Faith. St. James says that we should count it all a joy when trials come our way, because our Faith is put to the test (James 1:2).

And Peter assured the first Christians: "You must not think it unaccountable that you should be tested by fire. There is nothing extraordinary in what has happened to you. If you can have some share in the sufferings of Christ, *be glad*, because you will enjoy a much greater gladness when His glory is revealed" (1 Pet. 4:12-13).

Joy is the mark of a Christian—the mark of his Faith—the mark of the union of his Will with God's Will—the mark of his humility—and the mark of his Hope.

ON GOD, HIS HOME, AND HIS ANGELS

A true Christian begins to partake of joy — first in his own soul — and then he creates an atmosphere of joy for the sad hearts of others to be lifted up into the upper regions of Faith. He who lives in joy — creates joy and spreads joy; he gives the world a glimpse of Heaven.

Work in Heaven

The question of what we shall do in Heaven has puzzled millions of people throughout the centuries. Though we regard Heaven as a place of rest, it is certainly not a "do nothing" place.

The First Chapter of Genesis tells us of God's work as He created the world. At the end of each day He saw that it was good, and continued on to work until His design was completed.

When His greatest work on earth — Man — failed His original purpose, He continued to work in order to save what remained. All creation is the work of His Hands, and we marvel at His Power.

We often forget that everything we see, animate and inanimate, is a visual manifestation of the work of our invisible

God. We have become so accustomed to trees, mountains, sky, air, water, flowers, animals, vegetables, and people, that we no longer see them for what they are—God's work.

Jesus Himself came to work: "My food," He said, "is to do the Will of the One who sent me, and to complete His Work" (John 4:34).

God's original purpose was to create man to His Image and make him a son, but pride cut short His design, and man was only a reflection of His Creator's intellectual powers. God had to wait until man's pride reached out in humble supplication for help and deliverance.

Then it was that He sent His Son to complete the work which He had begun and man had interrupted. He made us Adopted Sons through the merits and sufferings of His Beloved Son.

When He came "unto His own and His own did not receive Him," He appealed to His works as proof of His mission. "The works My Father has given Me to carry out, these same works of Mine testify that the Father has sent Me" (John 5:36).

As great as His miracles were, the greatest work Jesus performed was the sanctification of souls, and the complete change that His life and doctrines made in the souls of men. And so it is with us. Though we may be blessed with charisms, if we are not changed into Jesus as we utilize these gifts, it is nothing; we have failed in our most important work.

It may be well for us to examine the word "work" before we go on. The word "work" normally means exertion, fatigue, and physical effort—all geared towards the accomplishment of a goal. The goal is the preservation of life, as we produce food to eat, clothing to wear, money to use, luxuries to buy, and possessions to hold. The very thought of work in Heaven is distressing, because physical work is something we dread to begin and long to end.

But the physical work that is necessary to maintain life is the lowest type of work. There is Intellectual work by which we acquire knowledge, to store in our Memory or to give to others. There is also Spiritual work, by which we are not only enlightened but changed.

In fact, all work has the power to change. It changes things and it changes people. The difference lies in the fact that while both physical and intellectual work changes things, spiritual works change souls.

Changing and transforming souls is the greatest work of all—the greatest work in our individual souls and in the souls of others. Jesus told us this when He said to His Apostles, "Whoever believes in Me will perform the same works as I do Myself; he will perform even greater works" (John 14:12).

What are these greater works? We know that Jesus performed many miracles to prove His Divinity, but though many believed in Him, He had few followers. It was the Apostles, after Pentecost, who converted three thousand in one day. These converts were more than believers — they were followers. They banded together into a community, shared their material and spiritual possessions, and lived as one heart and soul.

They had their problems, both within and without, but they worked towards a communal and individual imitation of Jesus, to the edification of their neighbor and the world.

The Apostles performed the same miracles Jesus performed, but they were given the work of building His Church — a Church that the gates of hell would not prevail against — a Church that would bear the fruit of sanctity throughout the ages — and that is the greatest work of all.

Spiritual work is not the only work, but it is the greatest. It is also the one most neglected on earth. The first Christians did both physical and mental work, but they added spiritual work, and this work influenced everything they did and everything they learned. It was that missing link that made their burdens easier and turned darkness into light.

If our workload is unbalanced by an overemphasis on physical or mental work, we shall have within us a kind of vacuum that no human activity or thought will ever fill.

This also applies to "good works." "If I give all I possess, and have not love, it is nothing" (1 Cor. 13:3). If the good works we perform are not motivated by a deep love for Jesus, and a desire to be like Him, then they lack the spiritual dimension: the vacuum is not filled, it is increased.

So many Christians complain that they feel empty even though they go to church and perform good works. It is because these works have never passed the physical and intellectual stages—they are believers and do the things of believers, but they are not "followers." They do not give Him their heart, mind, soul, and strength; they merely carry out a duty, the performance of which is done more out of fear than out of love. Every "follower" is a believer, but, unfortunately, every believer is not a follower.

A believer "does things," and in so doing, performs physical work. He has a belief in Jesus as Lord, so he performs an intellectual work. But when his Faith begins to demand a change in his life patterns, he often stops short. The exertion is too great, the time too long—he is overcome by spiritual inertia, and he does not enter into the greatest work of all—spiritual work.

What shall he do when God calls forth his soul from his body, and his physical capabilities are gone? His intellectual abilities, dulled by the absorption in the "things" that are past, must now continue to work in a place in which he is a stranger—a place his intellect has never roamed, his spirit never rested. What shall he do?

Paul answered this question, when he told us in the Epistle to the Corinthians, that "on the foundation of Christ we could build in gold, silver, and jewels, or in wood, grass, and straw." But then Paul realized that there are many souls who have never rejected God, and though they believed in Him as Savior, they never loved Him enough to change. Of these, Paul says, "That day will begin with fire, and the fire will test the quality of each man's work. The one whose structure stands up to it, he will get his wages (Heaven); if it is burnt down, he will be the loser, and though he is *saved himself*, it will be as one who has gone through fire" (1 Cor. 3:12-15).

Scripture often refers to the purification of the soul as a fire. Yes, though many accept life's trials as followers of the Master, and run into His arms at death, having become beautiful images of Jesus, there are others who were never changed into Jesus during their lifetime. They believed in Him and observed His Law, but a great portion of their soul was kept for themselves, and so at death they are saved but are not purified. Paul says these people will have time and a place to change — they will be as one who has gone *through* fire.

The word "through" indicates a place, and "fire" indicates a kind of purification. Yes, for those of us who believed but neglected our "spiritual work" to change, God's Mercy will purify us, for we cannot enter the Kingdom until we are sons in word and deed.

The greatest work we have is in our souls, because the extent to which we influence mankind depends upon the fruit Jesus bears in us. Like love, this work will continue on in Heaven. Though our capacity is set at death, we shall continue to learn, and to utilize that knowledge, in the Third Heaven.

In Heaven, we shall look down upon those we love on earth and pray for them. Our prayers in Heaven shall be totally unselfish and united to God's Will. They will not be mixed with fear, uncertainty or hesitation. We will ask, and we will know the reason why some of our prayers are not answered, and we will marvel at His Love and Wisdom.

God will often give us permission and power to help those on earth by invisibly directing their ways to the path of God. We will be able to fight the evil spirits as they tempt those we love. We will fight as sons of God—powerful and unafraid, dispelling those enemies of God, and triumphantly paving the way for those still in the earthly Kingdom to travel in peace. We will continue to work for the Kingdom until every last sheep is in the fold.

We have an example of this in the Book of Daniel. We read that the Archangel Gabriel, who was given the charge over a nation to aid it and protect it, was finding opposition from another Angel whose nation was a rival to Gabriel's charge (Dan. 10:13-19).

We read this amazing account with a spirit of incredulity, but this is only because we lack an understanding of the Love and Power of God. In our pride, we reject any concept of pure spirits, and when we read of them working for our salvation, we look upon these accounts as fairy tales.

Gabriel had been sent by God to tell Daniel about the coming struggle between Israel and their pagan neighbors.

ON GOD, HIS HOME, AND HIS ANGELS

The prophecy of the Angel was one that the guardians of these pagan nations feared, for it might lessen the time of their charges' repentance.

The Prince of Persia was desperately biding time for his nation to repent, and so he resisted Gabriel. This indicates that the fate of nations is something known only to God, and as long as God's Will was hidden from them, these Angel Guardians persevered in interceding and protecting their charges.

When Gabriel left to deliver his message to Daniel, he asked the great Angel Michael to take his place while those great Princes interceded before the Most High for their charges.

We feel we are given a look into Heaven as we read this — a Heaven filled with spirits totally given to God and yet interested in our earthly welfare. We will also be interested in our brothers' welfare on earth, and we shall pray for them with love and concern.

Unlike our interest on earth, our heavenly concern will be based on perfect knowledge of their condition and sufferings, and how these sufferings increase their eternal glory. We will work for their salvation, and perform whatever task is assigned to us by God in this regard.

Jesus gave us some indication of this when He gave us the parable of the talents. He was speaking of the Kingdom of Heaven, and He said it was like a man who went abroad and entrusted his property to his servants. "To one he gave five talents; to another, two; and to a third, one; each in proportion to his ability" (Matt. 25:15).

When the master came back, he asked an account of the talents he had given to his servants. The one who had been given five, had gained another five, and the master said, "Well done, good and faithful servant; you have shown you can be faithful in small things, I will trust you *with greater*; come and join in your master's happiness" (Matt. 25:23).

The remarkable thing about this parable is that Jesus is speaking of the Third Heaven. First, He explains that we must render an account for all the gifts and graces He has bestowed upon us. But then He speaks of the reward. The work we accomplished in this world is considered "small" compared to the "greater" work He shall entrust to us in the Kingdom.

If we have been faithful with the things that pass, He will entrust us with spiritual things, which are higher and greater. We shall begin this greater work in Heaven as we enter into His happiness.

ON GOD, HIS HOME, AND HIS ANGELS

One cannot read the Book of Revelation without being conscious of a tremendous amount of activity in Heaven. The Most High Lord sends Angels to punish the wicked with a variety of plagues. There is in this Book an awareness of God sending His servants on various missions for the good of the Kingdom.

It is part of God's Goodness to let us share in His Attributes.

Though He is our very life, He has given us a Will so we may share in His Power. Though we cannot say "Jesus" without His Spirit, He wants us to use Faith and our Reason to reach Him. Though we cannot be good without Him, He desires us to love as He loves. Though our strength comes from Him, He wants us to rejoice over the fruits of our labor.

He wants us to experience His joy after creation, when He finished His work and saw that it was good. There is a satisfaction after a job well done that words cannot express. And so in Heaven, we shall continue to work—work without effort or fatigue, work without fear of failure, work at the things we are best suited for, with all of Heaven to share in our continuous success.

The "small" work we have managed to do on earth, in the sweat of our brow, will be turned to great things in perfect joy. We shall do things we never dreamed of, with ease and alacrity. There will be a variety of work to suit our talents and personalities, and all this without the jealousy or envy of our fellowmen.

All of Heaven will be a hundred percent behind all we do, and rejoice at its success. The Book of Revelation tells us that in Heaven we shall "stand in front of God's Throne and *serve* Him day and night in His Sanctuary" (Rev. 7:15).

To serve is to work, and the work we do here, so mixed with pride, ambition, fatigue, and exertion, will be changed into effortless, tireless, selfless, and undistracted work.

We must not compare the work of Heaven with the work or talents we have on earth. The kind of work we have here is necessary for this material world. The talents we possess are also geared towards our earthly existence.

We often look at Heaven through the eyes of this world and we become confused. To most of us, Heaven is a place of eternal rest—an absence of work—a place of lulled sleep.

But this is not the Heaven we see in Scripture, and as we change places—earth to Heaven; change characteristics—self to Jesus; change names—our own for a new one; so we shall change work—earthly to Heavenly.

As we are changed, our capabilities, talents, and powers will be changed. Everything will be new and glorious, especially our work.

Even in this life, there are times when necessity or circumstances bring out hidden talents. We are able to do things we never thought we could. We seem to rise to the occasion and exhibit what we think are new talents, but are really only talents that were buried for want of opportunity. Suddenly, a new world opens up to us and we can do things with an ease we never thought possible. From the depths of our being, there arises a new ability that gives us assurance and confidence.

There are other times in life when God gives us *new* talents and abilities to meet new circumstances. During a war, for example, people are able to do things they never did before or after the war is over. It seems they have capabilities that are temporary—suited for a particular need and time. When the need is over, the talent seems to disappear. God does this so quietly and lovingly that we hardly notice it. We are only conscious that we rose to the occasion, but we do not know how.

And so it will be in Heaven. It will all be new and different, but God will bring out or put into our souls whatever we need for that place. The "One who sits on the Throne will spread His tent over us" (Rev. 7:15), and we shall do as He does, see as He sees, know as He knows, and love as He loves—we shall truly do the works of God.

Social Life in Heaven

When we speak of a social life, we speak of people, companionship, friendship, banquets, feasts, family ties, and communal living.

God created us to enjoy all these things. They are part and parcel of our human nature and our human existence.

Because our human nature is elevated by a participation in the Divine Nature, we are sons of God—but we are still human. We shall never be pure spirit by nature, for at the General Judgment we shall rise from the grave and our body will be reunited to our soul.

Our human nature will live, glorified and God-like, forever and ever.

ON GOD, HIS HOME, AND HIS ANGELS

We will look at each category mentioned above, and see how it will be in Heaven.

COMPANIONSHIP AND FRIENDSHIP

Because God is our life in Heaven, we shall have the most ideal friendship with everyone. There will not be one person who will not be our "best" friend and companion. We will all love one another in the same way God loves us.

This is why the New Commandment is so important on earth. When the Heaven within us reaches out to those around us, we begin on earth what we shall do eternally in Heaven—Love.

Though it will be easier to love in Heaven because everyone there is lovable, still in this world to love everyone, friend or foe, makes for as much of Heaven on earth as we can have. For to love an enemy *here* may make him a friend *there*, and we are bound to help everyone to the place God has destined for him. If they reject God and are separated from Him for all eternity, it must not be our fault.

We must make every effort to let our neighbor begin to feel the unselfish love of Heaven in this valley of tears.

In Heaven our friendship will not be determined by our social status or intellectual level, even though there are many mansions in our Father's house. We will not all have the same degree of glory or light, but this will not be the criteria for our friendship as it is on earth.

No matter how great anyone's glory is in Heaven, or how small our own, the difference will never interfere with our friendship.

For our friendship, based on God, will be sincere, secure, deep, and closely united to every great mind in Heaven. These intellectuals will share their lights with us in a most loving way, without the patient condescension we feel on earth when we attempt to make friends with those above us.

The humility in Heaven is so great that no one looks "down" upon anyone. We will see each other in God, and in each one of us there will be facets of God's perfections that are beautiful to behold. Each virtue or talent our neighbor exhibits will add to the joy of our friendship, because we will find in each other new opportunities to praise God for His Mercy and Power in our regard.

We will never suffer from jealousy in Heaven, and so our friendships will always be secure. We will see that everything good comes from God, and His Goodness diffuses itself into minute particles in every soul, so all the beauty and talents our neighbor possesses are only tiny reflections of our great God. We are like treasure hunters in Heaven—we seek, rather than run away from, the talents of others—in order to praise the Beauty and Mercy of God.

The deepest friendship on earth is often destroyed by misunderstanding. Rash judgment and pride can cause wounds that never heal, and we feel in our souls a sense of loss and emptiness that nothing can fill. A real friend, one who loves us as we are, and through every adversity, is rare. We are blessed by God if we find one, and that kind of friend is more valuable than riches.

But in Heaven, everyone will be that kind of friend. And what is more important, we will be that kind of friend to everyone there. Though it is only on earth that adversity tests friendship, in Heaven we shall all reap the fruits of that test, and we shall love and be loved for all eternity.

We cannot speak of the friendships in Heaven without wondering about those earthly friends we may not find there. Will their absence mar our joy in that place of bliss? What will our feelings be when and if we find a relative, a parent, a husband, a wife, or children, not in Heaven?

To answer that question, we must first ascertain the basis of friendship and love on earth. It is difficult to love as God loves, and so most of the time we love our neighbor for selfish reasons. This is often true in family life, and the cold indifference in some families today proves the existence of this sad kind of love. We love, not for God's sake, or because we see Him in them, but for our own sakes.

Love, worthy of the name, must be unselfish. It must be rooted in God, but most of us do not love in that way. As soon as a relative or friend demands more from us than he gives, our love grows cold. Because of this, we think that when we find someone who gives more than he receives from us, life without him would be unbearable. In reality, however, we love the service rendered more than the person who renders it.

God does not love in this way, and we should love as He loves. He loves us as we are even when we offend Him, because He is good, not because we are good. His love pursues us until that time or day when we totally reject Him. And even in letting us go, He shows love, because He permits us to do what pleases us.

It is difficult to understand anyone rejecting God and choosing evil, and yet daily life proves this all too often. In giving us free will, God has given us the power to choose what we love the most, for all eternity. It is possible after a life of sin to desire to hate and to be evil forever. Pride can make one choose self over God, choose hate over love, and choose evil over good.

Because of this, God has eternal enemies, who will also be our enemies forever. On earth, our love for a friend may have been based on some quality we thought he possessed in himself—beauty, wealth, poise, etc. But what we did not realize was that everything good in him was from God. It is a part of God in him that we loved. If the person we loved had only a veneer of goodness and finally rejected God, we would then see him as he really is in himself. Everything good, kind, and lovable would be stripped away for all eternity—and this by the soul's own choice, not God's.

So the person whom we may have thought absolutely necessary to our eternal happiness, we shall find hating us with an eternal hatred, possessing a Will forever set in rejecting God and us. There will be no way to love that person.

When Christ gave us the Commandment to love as He loves, He asked us to love everyone on earth in Him. We are to pray for those who injure us, and do good to those who hate us.

By doing this, we prevent ourselves from becoming hateful, and we provide an opportunity for an enemy to see God's Mercy and Goodness in us. We afford our neighbor the chance to repent and find God, but at the same time we respect his free will to reject us if he so chooses.

Like God, we extend love to our neighbor by concern and good deeds, but always leaving his Will free to accept or reject our love.

And so in Heaven we may find people whom we thought were our enemies, waiting to say "thank you" for showing them the Mercy and Compassion of God on earth. On the other hand, we may find those we thought were friends, forever separated from God in hell, because the goodness they possessed was only a veneer, worn thin through pride and selfishness, and turned into hatred.

We will be changed into Love and they will be changed into Hate. We will not miss them and they will not miss us, for the gulf between us will be unsurpassable. Those in Heaven will love God and one another in God. Those in hell will hate one another and themselves in pride.

Hell is not a pleasant place to look at, but we must understand that our happiness, joy, and love in Heaven are incapable of ever being marred or lessened by anyone in hell.

We must radiate Jesus to everyone we meet on earth, so that, seeing Him in us, they will desire to be with Him for all eternity.

BANQUETS AND FEASTS

Will there be banquets and feasts in Heaven? Yes, for even in this world Jesus used a Supper to institute the Holy Eucharist. On an occasion of unity and comradeship, He gave us His Body to eat and His Blood to drink.

The very word "feasting" gives the heart a sense of joy and expectation. It is a time when our souls are caught up in another world—a world of joy. It is a time when sorrows and trials are put aside, and we revel in the companionship of dear friends who rejoice with us, eat with us, and share with us.

In the Gospel of St. Luke, Jesus told us to be "dressed for action and have our lamps lit" because we do not know the hour when the Master will come and knock at our door. "Happy those servants whom the Master finds awake when He comes. I tell you solemnly, He will put on an apron, sit them down at table, and wait on them" (Luke 12:35, 37).

What a beautiful picture of death! To celebrate our coming home, all of Heaven will feast. On earth, the first thing we do when we meet a friend long overdue, is to invite him to dinner. We express love when we want someone to share our table with us.

And when Jesus comes to take us Home, and He finds us ready and waiting, He will express His deep Love by a banquet—a banquet at which He Himself will serve us—a feast beyond our wildest dreams.

All the nice little things we do on earth to express friendship and love, are mere shadows compared to the way love is manifested in Heaven. We have a tendency to think this material world is a place to rest, a place where we find perfection.

Yet, just the opposite is true. It is in Heaven that we shall find the things of earth were so imperfect and clumsy. We are fortunate in this valley of tears to have a friend invite us to dinner, who sincerely wants to have us or does not consider such an occasion an imposition.

ON GOD, HIS HOME, AND HIS ANGELS

Jesus warned us of this when He told us not to invite people to dinner who can invite us back (Luke 14:12). And St. Paul urged the first Christians to be hospitable, for hospitality was a mark of a real Christian (Rom. 12:13).

Yes, Jesus spoke often of meals, and He spent much time eating with His Apostles. Even after His Resurrection, He prepared breakfast for them at the Sea of Tiberias, and ate fish and honey with them in the Upper Room, to prove He had risen.

We cannot be sure what kind of food there will be at the feasts of Heaven, but we have three examples of the value of that food in Scripture.

We learn in the Book of Kings how Elias, running away from Jezebel, laid down under a furze tree. An Angel of the Lord appeared to him and gave him two scones to eat. The scones were so nourishing that Elias walked forty days and forty nights on the strength of that food (1 Kings 19:8).

Jesus Himself was strengthened by an Angel in the Garden of Gethsemane. The text does not say "encouraged" as one would do by words, but "strengthened" as one who was given food (Luke 22:43-44).

We also find in the Book of Tobias that the great Archangel Raphael told Tobit and his son that he had only appeared to eat the earthly food they gave him, for he had another food that they know nothing about (Tob. 12:19).

One day Jesus gave His Apostles courage by telling them of the reward to come. He said to them: "I confer a Kingdom on you, just as My Father conferred one on Me; you will eat and drink at My Table in My Kingdom, and you will sit on thrones to judge the Twelve Tribes of Israel" (Luke 22:28-30).

Jesus was speaking of the honor and dignity the Apostles would have in Heaven. As the First Class passengers eat at the Captain's table, so the Apostles would sit with their Master at His Table. And so shall we if we have been faithful to Him during our earthly sojourn.

We are assured of this in the Book of Revelations. "Look," Jesus said, "I am standing at the door, knocking. If one of you hears Me calling and opens the door, I will come in to share his meal, side by side with him" (Rev. 3:20).

God has put great significance on meals. The Passover sacrifice was a meal, eaten in haste, in memory of the night of the Exodus from Egypt. Jesus took the opportunity of a Passover meal to give us Himself until the end of time. "Do this," He said, "in memory of Me" (Luke 22:19).

ON GOD, HIS HOME, AND HIS ANGELS

Who is to say that when we meet Jesus face to face in death, we shall not celebrate that grand occasion by sitting with Him at table in His Kingdom? Do we not celebrate a loved one's return home by a festal meal? Many of us will be traveling for many years before we hear the call to go Home, but when we arrive, there will be great rejoicing at the table of the Lord.

Isaiah gave us a comforting imagery of judgment when he said, "Yahweh Sabaoth will prepare for all peoples a banquet of rich foods, a banquet of fine wines, of food rich and juicy" (Isa. 25:6). May we be found worthy to share this feast with our Triune God!

FAMILY TIES AND COMMUNAL LIVING

We have already touched upon the joys of being with loved ones in Heaven, but we must look at another aspect of that joy to understand our relationships in Heaven—Communal Living.

Being a member of a family does not necessitate communal living. Many families live separate lives and are joined together by name only.

We do not understand that every human being is a brother or sister because we share the same Father. We often live isolated and lonely lives in the midst of family and friends, with no real concern or love for anyone. We become "loners" in a crowd, and the desert around us is bleak indeed. We feel no comradeship or companionship with anyone, and we become walled-in human beings, unable to give or receive.

If we manage any friendships, it is with only a chosen few, who think as we think and do as we do. We are seldom "all things to all men" because we lack a proper understanding of the words "brother" and "friend". Our relationship with others is often on the servant level—meaning, we look down on their abilities as inferior to our own. We have nothing in common with them, so we ignore them.

It shall not be so in Heaven. We will have a personal love and consideration for each one there. We shall be deeply interested in one another, as real brothers and friends should be. And so, there will be a real family bond between us—an all-for-one and one-for-all attitude. We will possess that all-embracing love that includes everyone and excludes no one. It will be founded in God and never waver or lessen for all eternity.

Jesus gave us a glimpse into this family bond in Heaven when He answered the question of the Sadducees, who asked

Him about the woman with seven husbands. According to their all too human way of reasoning, the poor woman was going to have a problem in Heaven.

Jesus looked at them sadly, and answered, "Is not the reason why you go wrong, that you understand neither the Scriptures nor the Power of God? For, when they rise from the dead, men and women do not marry; no, they are like the Angels in Heaven" (Mark 12:24-25).

In Heaven, we shall be like the Angels, not by nature but by our total love for God and one another. On earth we had friends, parents, and relatives, who were interdependent upon one another for love and support. But in Heaven our happiness is dependent only upon God, and though we will know and love our dear ones in Heaven, our family ties will be enlarged to include everyone.

Jesus told a crowd one day that anyone who did the Will of His Father in Heaven was His brother, sister, and mother (Matt. 12:50). If this is true of Jesus, it is also true of us. We will be everything to everyone, with a feeling of belonging to one another.

There will be no prejudice to mar the happiness of our family life in Heaven, no social barriers to overcome, no feuds or jealousy to endure. Because we will all be one heart and one soul in God, we shall enjoy the most perfect cordial affection for everyone, and each one there will be as a brother, sister, mother, husband, and wife to everyone.

The time of testing will be over, and we shall reap the fruits of virtue for all eternity.

Clothing in Heaven

It may be difficult for many of us, who have an ethereal concept of Heaven, to think of clothing in Heaven. On earth, vanity and clothing are so often synonymous that we prefer to think of Heaven as a place where invisible spirits speak to one another in some intuitive manner, completely void of the joy of sight.

On earth, the quality of clothing we wear is dependent upon our social status. In Heaven, the kind and beauty of our clothing will be dependent upon the virtue we practiced on earth.

Each virtue will be represented by dress, color, and beauty, and all of Heaven will know, by looking at us, exactly how we glorified God on earth.

We have an example of this in the Book of Revelation. The Church of Sardis had not been faithful to the Gospel that had been preached to them. To reprimand them and wake them up, the Lord said, "There are a few in Sardis, it is true, who have kept their robes from being dirtied, and they are fit to come with Me, dressed in white. Those who prove victorious will be dressed, like these, in white robes" (Rev. 3:4-5).

White symbolizes purity, victory, and joy. The fact that white is symbolic, does not negate the reality of clothing in Heaven. The clothing is real though the color symbolizes a particular virtue.

The clothing in Heaven will not be of the coarse cloth that moths consume. The cloth and colors there will be different and of greater brilliance because they were purchased, not with money, but with pain, sacrifice, virtue, and often — Blood.

"Do you know who these people are, dressed in white robes, and where they come from? These are the people who have been through the great persecution, and, because they have washed their robes white again in the Blood of the Lamb, they now stand in front of God's Throne" (Rev. 7:14-15).

At the Transfiguration, Peter was notably taken back by the change in Christ's clothing. 'There, in their presence, He was transfigured: His clothes became dazzling white, whiter than any earthly bleacher could make them" (Mark 9:2-3).

It is significant that Peter would notice what many would consider a minor detail. Jesus did not become transparent as we often consider those in Heaven to be. His clothing changed; it did not disappear. St. Peter relived this episode when he conveyed it to Mark. He wanted to tell us it was a white he had never seen before. The only way he could express it was to say it was dazzling, and whiter than any bleach could make it.

In every Resurrection account of the appearance of Angels, we read of the same dazzling white robes — a white that is recognizable as such, but so superior to anything we have on earth that it is beyond comparison. It is ever white, eternally new, forever pure.

The virtue of purity will have a special place in Heaven. "There in front of the Throne they were singing a new hymn — a hymn that could only be learnt by the hundred and forty-four thousand.... These are the ones who have kept their virginity and not been defiled with women; they follow the Lamb wherever He goes" (Rev. 14:3-4).

Are those who have been given the gift to keep their virginity the only ones dressed in dazzling white? No, all those who have been faithful or repentant will be clothed in new garments. "His bride is ready and she has been able to dress herself in dazzling white linen, because her linen is made of the good deeds of the Saints" (Rev. 19:8).

Is white the only color our clothing shall have? Shall we all be dressed in long white robes, indistinguishable from one another for all eternity? No, for purity and faithfulness are not the only virtues.

There is the red of suffering and pain, the gold of love, the diamonds of zeal, the green of hope, the blue of gentleness, the silver of goodness, the violet of fidelity, the crimson of martyrdom, and the varied jewels of little sacrifices known to God alone.

We shall all shine out in varied colors and clothing, radiating the image of Jesus in different ways, and giving glory to the Father for His Mercy and Love.

The Prophet Daniel was astounded at the beauty of the Archangel Gabriel, and he tried to describe him by saying, "I saw a man dressed in linen, with a girdle of pure gold round his waist; his body was like beryl, his face shone like lightning, his eyes were like fiery torches, his arms and his legs had the gleam of burnished bronze" (Dan. 10:6).

In his vision of Heaven, St. John saw twenty-four elders sitting on thrones, dressed in white robes, with golden crowns on their heads (Rev. 4:4). The crowns are symbols of their authority, just as a crown on an earthly monarch is a sign of his authority. Each one of us in Heaven will be attired in the clothing that depicts our union with God. It will be beautiful beyond compare, and we will be amazed that God has given so much for so little.

The least act of kindness in this life will enhance our heavenly glory, and make us more beautiful to behold.

The beauty emanating from the Throne of God will reflect in each one of us, like the morning sun in a clear lake.

"And I saw a Throne standing in Heaven, and the One who was sitting on the Throne, and the Person sitting there, looked like a diamond and a ruby. There was a rainbow encircling the Throne and this looked like an emerald" (Rev. 4:3).

We shall have all this because "He loves us and has washed away our sins with His Blood, and made us a line of kings, priests to serve His God and Father" (Rev. 1:5-6).

Music and Beauty in Heaven

There are all kinds of music, and each one of us hears that particular kind that rejoices his heart. It may be different than anyone else's, but it is music nonetheless.

- There is the music of nature, ringing out the creative powers of God.
- There is the music of instruments to enliven the emotions and make one sing to the Lord.
- There is the music of silence — quiet, and filled with the thunder of His Presence.
- There is the music of pain, off beat and polyphonic, but nonetheless a beautiful hymn of resignation to God's Will.
- There is the music of loneliness, often sad and plaintive, but a hymn of sacrifice, a tune of the emptying of a vessel, sounding to Heaven and crying out to be filled.

- There is the music of the heart that cannot be expressed by words or tones, but can be seen on the face of the one who sings its melody.
- There is the music of light as it shines on the soul, reaching out to find and understand its Creator.
- There is the music of accomplishment, especially when we have overcome some sin or fault, the conquering of which has made us more like Jesus.

All these kinds of music make up a symphony of our lives. The last movement of our concert shall be played and sung in Heaven, when the tone and melody will be perfect, and all of Heaven will listen as we strum our own hymn of praise. "Above the Heavens is Your Majesty chanted by the mouths of children."(Ps. 8:1) "You have turned my mourning into dancing; You have stripped off my sackcloth and wrapped me in gladness; and now my heart, silent no longer, will play You music; Yahweh, my God, I will praise You forever" (Ps. 30:11-12).

St. John saw all those who had fought evil and won the battle. He said, "They all had harps from God, and they were singing the hymn of Moses" (Rev. 15:2-3).

ON GOD, HIS HOME, AND HIS ANGELS

The music in Heaven is so great that St. John was amazed when it suddenly stopped. "The Lamb then broke the Seventh Seal, and there was silence in Heaven for about half an hour" (Rev. 8:1).

It seems that the coming of God into John's vision was preceded by silence — the silence of the Great Presence — a time when all of Heaven is hushed at the Presence of its Lord.

At another time, John heard a great sound in Heaven — the sound of a huge crowd singing, "Alleluia! Victory and Glory and Power to our God!" They sang again and then prostrated themselves before the Throne, saying, "Amen, Alleluia!" (Rev. 19:1-3).

It must have sounded like the Angels who sang to the Shepherds on the hillside when Jesus was born. They sang a message to mankind — a message of peace and salvation — a message of hope to a world in despair.

The first Christians were very much aware of the witnessing quality of music, whether the music be the kind that is heard or the peaceful kind that is in the heart.

St. Paul told us to sing, not only with the spirit, but with the mind (1 Cor. 14:14). That silent song of the heart, or the mind, must begin here and continue on throughout eternity.

Even the ascetical St. James urged the first Christians to sing when they felt happy. If this is true in this life, how much more true is it of Heaven.

When we are all together in Heaven, we shall do what Paul urged the Ephesians to do: "Sing the words and tunes of the psalms and hymns when you are together, and go on singing and chanting to the Lord in your hearts, so that always and everywhere you are giving thanks to God, who is our Father, in the Name of our Lord Jesus Christ" (Eph. 5:19-20).

St. Paul wanted the Gospel to ring out in song on earth as it does in Heaven. "Let the message of Christ, in all its richness, find a *home* in you. ... With gratitude in your hearts, sing psalms and hymns and inspired songs to God" (Col. 3:16).

In Heaven, we shall sing in tunes, in heart and in mind, for there we shall see Everlasting Beauty face to Face, and we shall burst forth in songs unsung before — songs in the Spirit — spontaneous, free, flowing, rich in melody, pleasing to the ear, and personal.

We will sing, alone, of the Mercy of the Lord in our individual lives, and we shall sing, together, of His Victory and Power.

ON GOD, HIS HOME, AND HIS ANGELS

Those of us on earth who have been deprived of a beautiful voice, or those who were born deaf and dumb, will sing and hear the most beautiful of melodies.

The deaf will hear tones and songs that others will never hear, because God is just, and His Justice will make up to them for all the sounds and music they have never heard. We on earth look upon the deaf with sympathy, but in Heaven, where the last are first, their souls will be delighted with the most exquisite tones for all eternity. They will forget the sorrow of their earthly privation as soon as they hear a voice for the first time — the Voice of God!

Who could ever describe the ecstasy of that moment — the moment a person born deaf, dumb, or blind, dies and sees God, hears God, and speaks to God!

The beauty that a person born blind will see is beyond the capability of human words to express. To have been in darkness for so many years, and then suddenly to see the Heavenly Jerusalem "glittering like some precious jewel of crystal clear diamond" (Rev. 21:19), will far surpass the sorrow of their lives.

How true were the words of St. Paul when he said, "I think that what we suffer in this life can never be compared to the glory... which is waiting for us" (Rom. 8:18).

The walls of the City of Heaven are built of diamonds, the City itself of pure gold glittering like polished brass. The foundations are diamonds, emeralds, crystal, and gems that eye has never seen. Each gate is made of a single pearl, and the Light that eternally shines, bright and glorious, is God Himself (Rev. 21:15-26).

Though the poor, the crippled, the distressed, and the handicapped will rejoice in this sight in a very special way, all of us, rich and poor, who have been faithful, will find the Beauty of the Kingdom an ecstatic experience, filled with wonder and awe.

On earth, the most beautiful landscape becomes monotonous in time, but it will not be so in Heaven. The Beauty there will be ever changing so as to bring forth from our souls a never ending source of joy.

There will always be new things to see, because God is an Infinite, Eternal source of Beauty. Science hasn't even begun to plumb the secrets of our tiny world, and this is only a passing world. What shall it be like in Heaven where everything is forever, everything is perfect, everything is beautiful, and everyone full of God!

ON GOD, HIS HOME, AND HIS ANGELS

We shall be given the grace to see Him face to Face. We shall possess the Light of Glory. We shall see a great cloud with light around it, a fire from which flashes of lightning dart, and in the center a sheen like bronze. And then we shall see Something that looks like a sapphire; shaped like a throne, and high up on this throne we shall see One who looks like a man. He will look like fire and light, with a rainbow around the Throne (Ezek. 1:4-5, 26-28).

We will look at Him and He will look at us, and though Heaven will be filled with people, each one will feel he is there with God alone. There will be a very personal, loving relationship between God and ourselves. He will look at each one of us, and all our wishes and desires shall be fulfilled.

We would be annihilated by the sight of His Glory and His Love if He did not bestow upon us a special part of Himself, to withstand the great joy of that moment.

The grace we have in this world, invisible and unfelt, will blossom out suddenly, and we shall glow as He glows, be filled with Light as He is Light, and love as He loves. His Beauty will touch us and we, too, shall radiate with an eternal Beauty.

Knowledge in Heaven

"The knowledge that I have now is imperfect; but then I shall know as fully as I am known" (1 Cor. 13:12).

One of the most delightful experiences in Heaven will be the acquisition of knowledge. We will not be hampered by dull intellects and laborious methods of learning. We will know a truth, fully, clearly, and immediately, without effort, time, or fatigue, and we shall also know ourselves.

One of life's problems is the fact that we do not know ourselves. It seems the self-image and the people-image are totally opposed. We seldom believe a criticism, constructive or otherwise. We are more or less faultless as far as we are concerned, and resent the insinuations of our neighbors to the contrary.

It is possible to live a lifetime and never know oneself—or God. The reason for this is that we are uncomfortable at the sight of our faults and sins, and even when we tell them to God we manage to cloak them in such a way that they almost seem virtuous.

But in Heaven, when the mask we have worn is finally discarded, we shall know ourselves as we were on earth, praise

Him for His Mercy, and see our real self as it is in His sight, and praise Him for His Love.

We will no longer be afraid of ourselves, for all imperfections and evil inclinations will be gone. We will not have to struggle to know God's Will, for we shall be united to Him forever.

St. Paul assures us that our souls will be enlightened by God Himself: "Let there be light shining out of darkness, who has shone in our minds, to radiate the light of the knowledge of God's Glory—the Glory on the face of Christ" (2 Cor. 4:6).

There will be no more doubts in Heaven. We shall never see the end of new things to learn, and our lack of knowledge will never be frustrating as it is on earth. We will be content to know what God wants us to know, and we will be given new knowledge to delight our minds for all eternity.

All the mysteries of God in Scripture will be opened to us, and we shall understand clearly its interpretation, the symbolisms, and how everything fits together for the salvation of mankind.

We shall see how different passages affected our individual lives on earth, and how the Lord Jesus had each one of us in mind when He lived and died for our salvation.

We shall understand God's Infinity and Trinity, and we shall rejoice with exceeding great joy over the realization of the Mystery of God-made-Man.

Paul prayed for this knowledge on earth when he said, "May the God of our Lord Jesus Christ, the Father of Glory, give you a spirit of wisdom and perception of what is revealed, to bring you to full knowledge of Him" (Eph. 1:17). If this is possible in this life, how much more will it be so in the life to come?

Our very love for one another will be a source of knowledge. There are many wonderful virtues and talents in our neighbor that will increase our knowledge of God. "My prayer," St. Paul said, "is that your love for each other may increase more and more and never stop improving your knowledge and deepening your perception" (Phil. 1:9). There will be various facets of each other's holiness in Heaven that will increase our understanding of God and His Glory — beautiful qualities of soul that will shine like jewels to radiate His Beauty and Goodness for all Eternity.

We will understand the role we played in salvation history, and how many souls were influenced and drawn to God by our prayers and example. We will see them all, and they will be grateful to God for the graces He has given to us, and we shall be grateful for the graces He has given to them.

We will know all the things in this life that we wondered about, and many things in the next life that are completely new and wonderful.

Every instant of eternity will be fresh, new, and full of knowledge. We will have the joy of sharing that knowledge with one another. As one learns some new truth, he will share it with someone else, and together they will glorify God who gives such understanding to His children.

All the different sciences will be open to us, and we will laugh at the furrowed brows of the past as we wondered how the world came to be, and how man became a living soul. We will know the stars by name and understand their purpose and how they were made.

We will all know a universal language in Heaven, similar to the one the Apostles received at Pentecost when they were understood by more than three thousand. We will be able to converse with everyone, and be understood, no matter what language they spoke on earth.

And when we have finished with all the Mysteries of the universe, there will be new Mysteries to refresh our minds, for at every moment we shall have just begun.

Body and Soul in the Kingdom

We think of the calling forth of the soul from the body as death. In reality, it is merely a passing from one condition of life to another.

The early Christians called it sleep, because the body was in repose — no longer animated by its life-giving principle, the soul. Their passing was a birthday — a spiritual birthday — their first day in the Third Kingdom.

On earth, our life begins at conception. It is a sacred time — a time when God and nature work the miracle of life — the creation of body and soul. It is a time of silent wonder, a time of danger and suspense, a time of love and prayer, a time when parents and relatives wait for the day of accomplishment — the entering of a new life into the world.

We can compare our lifetime to the nine months in our mother's womb; it, too, is a preparation, a miracle of God's

Grace and our free will. It, too, is full of danger and suspense, love and prayer, pain and joy.

It takes only nine months to develop a human body, into which God has breathed a living soul, made to His Image, but it takes a lifetime of God's Grace and our free will to be transformed into Jesus.

By Baptism, the Holy Spirit takes up His abode in our souls, and St. Paul tells us in the Epistle to the Romans, "if the Spirit of Him who raised Jesus from the dead is living in you, then He who raised Jesus from the dead will give life to your own mortal bodies through His Spirit living in you" (Rom. 8:11).

We must give God our most prized possession — our Will — unite it to His, and, through the power of His Holy Spirit, be transformed into Jesus. To be called to such a dignity is a greater act of His Goodness than all creation.

The first Christians were so conscious of this privilege that they rejoiced over the sufferings of this world, and ever kept their hearts lifted up in Hope of what was to come.

And when the Transition finally came and they saw God face to Face, it was just like going home — beginning a new life — reaping the fruit of their years of toil.

The soul, made to resemble its God, will, if it has been faithful to Him, be united to Him forever. We have many proofs of this in Scripture. Jesus promised the Good Thief that on that very day he would be with Him in His Kingdom (Luke 23:43).

Before this, Jesus told the Sadducees, "Have you never read in the Book of Moses, in the passage about the Bush, how God spoke to him and said, I am the God of Abraham, the God of Isaac, and the God of Jacob? He is God, not of the dead, but of the living" (Mark 12:26-27). The souls of these great men were waiting for Redemption so they might go to the Kingdom with their Lord. We see Moses and Elias speaking to Jesus at the Transfiguration, talking to Him of the suffering to come (Mark 9:4).

We read in the Acts how Stephen gazed into Heaven and saw the Glory of God, and Jesus standing at His right hand. Scripture puts it beautifully when it says, "he knelt down and said aloud, 'Lord, do not hold this sin against them' and with these words he fell asleep" (Acts 7:60).

His body reposed and returned to the dust from which it was taken, but his soul, and the faculties that were so much a part of it—Memory, Understanding, and Will—began to enjoy the delights of the Kingdom.

And so it shall be with us. Our soul will enjoy the Vision of God. We call it Beatific because we shall see God as He is. The Great "I Am" will reach down and take us to Himself.

To see Him is to know Him, and so our souls will be flooded with an understanding of God that we never dreamed possible.

A third quality will be added to *Vision* and *Knowledge*, and that is, *Possession*. We shall possess God forever. We have arrived Home and will never leave that blessed place.

These three gifts (Vision, Knowledge, and Possession) our souls will enjoy until the day of the General Resurrection, when they will be reunited to our bodies.

St. Paul told the Philippians, "For us, our homeland is in Heaven, and from Heaven comes the Saviour we are waiting for, the Lord Jesus Christ, and He will transfigure these wretched bodies of ours into copies of His Glorious Body" (Phil. 3:20-21).

We need not worry about those bodies that have turned into dust, or were lost at sea. Each one of us is in the mind of God, and "instantaneously, in the twinkling of an eye, when the last trumpet sounds…the dead shall be raised, imperishable…

because our present perishable nature must put on imperishability, and this mortal nature put on immortality" (1 Cor. 15:52-53).

We must look at the Resurrected Jesus if we are to see the properties our glorified bodies will possess on that day of the General Resurrection.

Light is the first quality our body will receive. It will take on the clarity of the soul, since it is now subject to the soul. Our body will be luminous as the sun and beautiful to behold.

It will take on the Glory of the Lord, and its degree of brightness will depend upon our love for God. We shall be as bright stars. The Body of Jesus manifested this quality when It radiated light at the Transfiguration.

His Body also shone with Glory when He manifested Himself to Stephen, and to Paul by that blinding light that threw Paul off his horse and made him cry out, "Who are You, Lord?" (Acts 9:5).

St. Paul told the Corinthians, "The sun has its brightness, the moon a different brightness, and the stars a different brightness, and the stars differ from each other in brightness. It is the same with the resurrection of the dead…the thing that is sown is contemptible, but what is raised is glorious" (1 Cor.

15:41-42). "And we, who have been modeled on the earthly man will be modeled on the heavenly man" (1 Cor. 15:48). Our bodies will be as dazzling as the Angels that appeared to Prophets and Apostles, for we shall truly be like Him.

Like the Body of Jesus, our body will be *Incorrupt*. It will never again change, for, like the soul, it shall live forever. "When this perishable nature has put on imperishability, and when mortal nature has put on immortality, then the words of Scripture will come true: 'Death is swallowed up in victory. Death, where is your victory? Death, where is your sting?'" (1 Cor. 15:54-56).

We will never need to nourish the glorified body by food, even though it is capable of eating. This surprising aspect is evident in the Resurrection account of St. Luke. The Apostles were dumbfounded when Jesus stood in their midst, and to prove to them He had truly risen said, "Have you anything to eat?" And they offered Him a piece of grilled fish, which He took and *ate* before their eyes" (Luke 24:41).

The glorified body will retain all its senses, but these senses will no longer rule the soul as they so often did on earth. They will be purified and glorified forever under the rule of the Will, totally given to God.

Our body will never suffer from pain or disease or any other affliction. It will possess the most perfect health. It will be forever young and vibrant. We can only speculate as to age, but if we are to be copies of the Master, then we can safely surmise that we shall all look as we did, or would have looked, at the age of thirty-three.

Like the glorified Body of Jesus, our body will also have the power of Penetration. It will take on the quality of a spirit, permitting it to go through any material object.

Twice we read of this ability in the Gospel of St. John. "In the evening," John says, "of that same day, the first day of the week, the *doors were closed*…Jesus came and stood among them" (John 20:19).

"Eight days later, the disciples were in the house again, and Thomas was with them. The doors were closed, but Jesus came in and stood among them" (John 20:26).

And so it was when He rose. He walked through the sealed tomb—glorious and triumphant. St. Matthew tells us "there was a violent earthquake, and the Angel of the Lord, descending from Heaven, came and rolled away the stone, and sat upon it" (Matt. 28:2). The women were frightened, for the tomb was empty. Their Lord had already risen and had gone before them into Galilee.

The question arises that if we are in Heaven, body and soul, will there be any solid objects to penetrate? We do not know the answer, but we do know that when God raises the dead on the Last Day, we shall be free and unhampered, and no gift from God will be superfluous or useless.

The fourth quality our body shall have is Agility. It will travel with swiftness and ease, unhampered by gravity or physical laws. We need not ever again envy the birds in their flight.

Jesus manifested this quality even during His lifetime. One evening when the Apostles were at sea, a storm surprised them, and they saw the Master walking on the waters, They were frightened, but He said to them, "It is I. Do not be afraid." They were for taking Him into the boat, but in no time it reached the shore at the place they were making for (John 6:19-21).

These men were miles from shore, yet suddenly, by an act of the Master's Will, they arrived at their destination.

After the Resurrection, we find this quality of Agility manifested often. Jesus appears to Magdalen, then to Peter, then, suddenly, we find Him talking to the disciples going to Emmaus.

His movements were effortless and sudden, but always quiet, serene, and loving. He is always Divine, but still human. He manifested a beautiful thoughtfulness when He prepared breakfast for His Apostles on the shore of Tiberias. His forgiveness was sublime as He asked Peter three times if he loved Him. His Generosity was overflowing when He gave men the power to Baptize and thereby make other men sons of God. His Love was so burning He sent the Holy Spirit to live in our souls so He might be united to us.

Our souls in Heaven will see God, know God, and possess God, and be reunited to our bodies which will be refulgent with Light, Incorrupt, able to Penetrate any object, and Agile as a spirit.

Jesus promised us this when He said, "Do not be surprised at this, for the hour is coming when the dead will leave their graves at the sound of His voice: those who did good will rise again to life, and those who did evil to condemnation" (John 5:28-29).

We realize from this that it is not only the just who will rise from the dead. All those who have rejected God and whose souls have been in hell shall also rise from their graves at the sound of His Voice.

ON GOD, HIS HOME, AND HIS ANGELS

Their portion is the exact opposite of the just. They will never see the Face of God; they will never understand His Love, and never enjoy His Presence. Their souls are filled with hate, and when those souls are reunited to their bodies, instead of Light, they shall have Darkness; instead of immunity from pain, they shall have torment; instead of Penetration, they shall be constricted; instead of Agility, they shall move with difficulty; instead of being forever beautiful, they will be eternally grotesque; and the fire of hate shall burn in their hearts time without end.

All of this because they chose to do evil rather than good. They refused to put on the "new self." They refused "to kill everything in them that belonged only to earthly life: fornication, impurity, guilty passions, evil desires, and especially — greed, which is the same as worshipping a false god" (Col. 3:5).

We are all called by God to be holy, for Jesus told His disciples, "It is never the Will of your Father in Heaven that one of these little ones should be lost" (Matt. 18:14).

He made this statement after telling them how a good shepherd leaves his ninety-nine sheep and goes to seek a stray.

We must "put on a new self which will progress towards true knowledge the more it is renewed in the image of its Creator" (Col. 3:10). This is the Kingdom within us.

We are "God's chosen race, His saints; He loves us and so we must be clothed in sincere compassion, in kindness and humility, gentleness and patience. Bear with one another; forgive each other as soon as a quarrel begins" (Col. 3:12-13).

Like a rainbow in the sky, these virtues give Hope to our neighbor and enhance the Kingdom around us.

And when we have reached spiritual maturity, and our "faces reflect like mirrors the brightness of the Lord," then the "Spirit will say to the Bride—Come" and we shall sing with the Angelic choir, "Victory and glory and power to our God. Alleluia! Alleluia!" (2 Cor. 3:18; Rev. 22:17, 19:1).

Mother M. Angelica
(1923-2016)

Mother Mary Angelica of the Annunciation was born Rita Antoinette Rizzo on April 20, 1923, in Canton, Ohio. After a difficult childhood, a healing of her recurring stomach ailment led the young Rita on a process of discernment that ended in the Poor Clares of Perpetual Adoration in Cleveland.

Thirteen years later, in 1956, Sister Angelica promised the Lord as she awaited spinal surgery that, if He would permit her to walk again, she would build Him a monastery in the South. In Irondale, Alabama, Mother Angelica's vision took form. Her distinctive approach to teaching the Faith led to parish talks, then pamphlets and books, then radio and television opportunities.

By 1980 the Sisters had converted a garage at the monastery into a rudimentary television studio. EWTN was born. Mother Angelica has been a constant presence on television in the United States and around the world for more than thirty-five years. Innumerable conversions to the Catholic Faith have been attributed to her unique gift for presenting the gospel: joyful but resolute, calming but bracing.

Mother Angelica spent the last years of her life cloistered in the second monastery she founded: Our Lady of the Angels in Hanceville, Alabama, where she and her Nuns dedicated themselves to prayer and adoration of Our Lord in the Most Blessed Sacrament.